The Emerging 16–19 Curriculum

Policy and Provision

Jeremy Higham, Paul Sharp and David Yeomans

David Fulton Publishers

London

David Fulton Publishers Ltd
2 Barbon Close, London WC1N 3JX

First published in Great Britain by
David Fulton Publishers 1996

British Library Cataloguing in Publication Data

A catalogue record for this book is available from the British Library

ISBN 1-85346-389-2

Typeset by The Harrington Consultancy
Printed in Great Britain by BPC Books and Journals Ltd, Exeter

Contents

Acknowledgements

We wish to thank the schools, colleges, teachers and students who participated in the research upon which this book is based and the School of Education, University of Leeds, for funding the work.

Series Editor's Foreword

While much still needs to be done to improve our education system up to the age of 16, it is provision for young people aged 16 to 19 (and beyond) that is most in need of radical or (perhaps more realistically) constructive rethinking. As the authors of this major study point out, the 16 to 19 curriculum in many schools and colleges is an uncomfortable mixture of prestigious courses for some and low-status programmes for others. And it is this clear division between the academic and the vocational – in a system dominated by the 'beached whale' of A level – that is seen by many as preventing the provision of genuine equality of opportunity for all at the post-16 stage. It has indeed been argued by many commentators that the widening of access to all forms of higher education and lifelong learning can be achieved only by moves towards a more coherent, unitary and integrated public system of 16 to 19 education and training.

Drawing on their own research for this book in the final chapter looking at the way forward, the authors found very little support from students for a major reform of the post-16 curriculum. Teachers, on the other hand, could see the need for change – but very much along the comparatively cautious lines adopted in the interim report of Sir Ron Dearing's review of the framework of 16 to 19 qualifications. It is their (albeit qualified) support for Dearing's incremental and evolutionary approach, with its scope for facilitating bottom-up approaches to the reform of the post-16 curriculum, which enables the authors to end the book on a relatively positive and optimistic note.

Clyde Chitty
Birmingham
February 1996

QUALITY IN SECONDARY SCHOOLS AND COLLEGES SERIES

Series Editor: Clyde Chitty

This series publishes on a wide range of topics related to successful education for the 11–19 age group. It reflects the growing interest in whole-school curriculum planning together with the effective teaching of individual subjects and themes. There are also books devoted to management and administration, examinations and assessment, pastoral care strategies, relationships with parents and governors and the implications for schools of changes in teacher education. Titles include:

Active History in Key Stages 3 and 4
Alan Farmer and Peter Knight
1–85346–305–1

English and Ability
Edited by Andrew Goodwyn
1–85346–299–3

English and the OFSTED Experience
Bob Bibby and Barrie Wade (with Trevor Dickinson)
1–85346–357–4

Geography 11–16: Rekindling Good Practice
Bill Marsden
1–85346–296–9

Heeding Heads: Secondary Heads and Educational Commentators in Dialogue
Edited by David Hustler, Tim Brighouse and Jean Rudduck
1–85346–358–2

Learning to Teach: a Guide for School-Based Initial and In-Service Training
Julian Stern
1–85346–371–X

The Literate Imagination: Renewing the Secondary English Curriculum
Bernard T. Harrison
1–85346–300–0

Managing the Learning of History
Richard Brown
1–85346–345–0

Moral Education Through English 11–16
Ros McCulloch and Margaret Mathieson
1–85346–276–4

The New Teacher: An Introduction to Teaching in Comprehensive Education
Nigel Tubbs
1–85346–424–4

Partnership in Secondary Initial Teacher Education
Edited by Anne Williams
1–85346–361–2

School Improvement: What Can Pupils Tell Us?
Edited by Jean Rudduck, Roland Chaplain and Gwen Wallace
1–85346–393–0

Valuing English: Reflections on the National Curriculum
Roger Knight
1–85346–374–4

Introduction

Education and training policy for 16–19 year olds is the subject of much political and educational debate and discussion. We suggest some of the reasons for this widespread and consistent interest in the next chapter, but it is worth briefly reflecting more generally upon the important place which the 16–19 curriculum holds in education in England and Wales. The 16–19 curriculum contains some of the most prestigious elements of the school and college curriculum (academic qualifications) alongside other elements (vocational qualifications) which, while catering for large numbers of students, have been largely neglected by politicians and academic commentators alike for many years. It is this combination of the prestigious and the disregarded which makes the 16–19 curriculum an important and fascinating area of study. Fundamental battles over aims, form and content are fought out over 16–19 education and training in clashes of political and educational values.

In undertaking the research upon which this book is based we wanted to inform and illuminate the debate over the 16–19 curriculum, the results of which are likely to have far-reaching consequences well into the next century. It is worth noting that whereas twenty years ago only a small proportion of young people aged 16–19 stayed on in full-time education, more than two out of three 16 year olds now do so.

In a book about policy and practice it is necessary to do some conceptual ground-clearing concerning the meaning of these terms and the relationship between them. We view policy-making not as a linear, formulation–implementation process, but as involving complex processes of reinterpretation and recontextualisation at different levels. Thus, while decisions at national level in departments of state and associated agencies, and the contributions of prestigious national bodies such as the Confederation of British Industry (CBI) and the National Commission on Education and think-tanks such as the Institute of Public Policy Research (IPPR) are important and influential, we recognise that schools and colleges respond to a whole series of local, contextual factors as well as to national policy imperatives and debates. In addition, of course, schools and colleges are not merely reactive institutions, they also have their own histories, ethos and interests which actively shape policy. Within the institutions there are further divisions, debates and struggles for resources and power as internal policies are formulated and implemented. Thus it is the interplay of national, local and institutional level factors which help to determine the form and content of the 16–19 curriculum. To summarise, the relationship between policy and practice (and indeed determining where one ends and the other begins) is highly complex and operates on a number of levels and along several dimensions.

There is one further general observation on policy and practice worth making at this point. There is always a danger of an over-rational approach to policy analysis, as though policy-making consists of selection among a range of alternatives based upon a careful clarification of aims and values and weighing of evidence. We suggest that such rational calculations play only a part in the making of policy. For example, Duncan Graham, then chief executive of the National Curriculum Council, was reported as explaining that some subjects were omitted from the National Curriculum because 'people did not write them in when they were writing the Act because they did not have them in their own prep schools' (quoted in Ball, 1990, p134). If there is anything in this rather mischievous comment, and we suspect there might be, how much stronger must be the 'official memory' of the 1950s and 1960s sixth form? For many national and local policy-makers the most recent and perhaps strongest memory of their school days will be that of the academic school sixth form. We suggest there is a strong element of nostalgia in some of the contributions to the debates about the future of the sixth form which resonates with John Major's vision of a happier, or at least simpler, England of warm beer, cricket on the village green and spinsters cycling to church. Of course, the reality is that in the 1950s and 1960s only a small minority of 16–18 year olds actually attended the sixth forms of the public and grammar schools where General Certificate of Education (GCE) Advanced level (A level) study reigned supreme. However, this minority came to make up the overwhelming majority of the political, administrative and educational policy-making élites. Set against this nostalgia and traditionalism advocates of modernisation argue that the existing 16–19 curriculum, with its clear divisions between academic and vocational courses is anachronistic, dominated as it is by the 'beached whale' of A level, and that in the modern highly competitive world of the 1990s the sooner it is reformed out of all recognition the better. This is deemed to be essential if Britain is to be economically competitive in the twenty-first century. However, this modernisation scenario asserts causal connections between education generally, the 16–19 curriculum specifically and economic competitiveness not justified by the available evidence. Thus if the traditionalists are stuck in the past, the modernisers may be greatly over-claiming for the benefits which would flow from their proposals.

Therefore more subjective elements in policy-making should be borne in mind throughout the book and particularly with regard to Chapter 1, where we discuss some of the main strands of the debate about the 16–19 curriculum. While a recapitulation of this debate is clearly essential in order to contextualise the later chapters, and to update earlier accounts, our main interest has been in showing how a range of schools are responding to the national policy debate and are shaping their sixth form provision in the light of national policies, local circumstances and their own internal imperatives.

Thus, in much of what follows it is the voices of the teachers and the students which predominate. We make no apologies for this, indeed we see it as a strength of the book. In all the debates about the 16–19 curriculum, politicians, academics, employers and teacher organisations have all had much to say, but little has been heard from teachers and even less from students. This book aims to go some way to rectifying this omission. We believe it is important to do this because if recent attempts at educational reform have shown anything it is that national policy-makers ignore teachers' views at their peril, and while pre-16 students may be, to some extent, a 'captive audience', post-16 students do have at least some capacity to vote with their feet if what is offered is not to their liking.

The empirical data upon which the book is based were collected from schools in the six local education authority (LEA) areas in West and North Yorkshire (Leeds, Bradford, Kirklees, Calderdale, Wakefield and North Yorkshire) in 1993 and 1994. Questionnaires were sent to all schools of over 400 pupils, with sixth forms, requesting details of the sixth form curriculum, any recent changes and plans for the future. Seventy-one schools completed questionnaires, representing a response rate of 54 per cent. Some of the quantitative data in the following pages is drawn from this questionnaire survey and, where appropriate, we have also made use of publicly available national statistics.

In addition to the questionnaire survey, visits were made to a stratified sample of 20 schools. The schools visited were selected on the basis of: LEA/grant maintained/independent status; roll size; mixed or single sex intake. We also sought to obtain a balanced sample by taking into account the socio-economic characteristics of the catchment areas of the schools as well as their academic performance. We are confident that the sample visited is representative of schools with sixth forms within North and West Yorkshire and that it, like the questionnaire sample, reflects schools across England and Wales.

Within the schools we collected relevant curriculum and policy documents, most importantly sixth form prospectuses. We conducted semi-structured interviews with heads of sixth forms and, where possible and appropriate, with other staff responsible for elements of the curriculum, e.g. General National Vocational Qualifications (GNVQ) coordinators. We also conducted small group interviews with students from Year 11 and from the sixth form. With sixth formers we requested groups drawn from a range of courses, e.g. different A level and GNVQ courses. With Year 11 students we asked teachers to select students who were expected to follow a range of routes post-16, e.g. A level courses, GNVQ courses, attend college, leave school and enter employment and training. The interviews with staff and students were tape-recorded and later transcribed and analysed.

The structure of the book is as follows: in Chapter 1 we review the contextual influences on the 16–19 curriculum and trace some of the strands of the curriculum debate which has arisen over recent years. We focus on recent legislation affecting 16–19 education and summarise some of the major policy statements and reports on the curriculum. This leads us to outline the main questions, issues and problems which have emerged from the debate over the curriculum and provides a framework for the chapters which follow. In Chapter 2 we mainly draw on questionnaire and other quantitative data to provide an overview of the sixth form curriculum in the schools in terms of its constituent elements and the ways in which these have changed. Chapters 3 to 7 are the heart of the book and focus on the academic curriculum, the vocational curriculum and the core curriculum. For each we examine the patterns of provision, the ways in which these have changed, explanations for these changes and views of the future. For each chapter we contextualise developments in the schools through examination of national debates. It is important to emphasise that the division of the material in these chapters was taken mainly as a convenient means of presentation. We do not imply that the academic, vocational and core curricula were necessarily distinct in the schools. The degree of overlap and commonality between them are issues which are explored throughout the book. Still less do we imply that the academic/vocational division in the curriculum has some philosophical and epistemological justification, that again is one of the central issues in the whole debate about the 16–19 curriculum. In Chapter 8 we focus on the information and guidance available to students in Year 11 as they prepare to choose which route to follow post–16. Again, in addition to data from our own study, we make use of other sources to review this currently controversial issue. We end the book by reviewing our own evidence and that from other sources and by outlining significant trends in the 16–19 curriculum. Finally we consider the implications of our findings for the future policy and practice of the 16–19 curriculum and offer our own thoughts on how this might be constructed.

CHAPTER 1

Contextual Influences on the 16–19 Curriculum

A level is widely understood by parents and by industry and by the higher education system to which it is a gateway. Why mess about with something which is so good.
(Michael Fallon, formerly Minister of State, Department of Education and Science)

The A level remains like some beached whale, unresponsive to what precedes it and increasingly irrelevant to what follows it.
(Leslie Wagner, formerly Director, Polytechnic of North London, now Principal, Leeds Metropolitan University)

Advanced GNVQs will increasingly be seen as relevant, exciting and a worthwhile route either to employment or higher education.
(Noel Kershaw, Principal, and Ken Gadd, Director of Curriculum Development, Yeovil College)

Compared with the comparable qualifications of our continental neighbours, GNVQs appear lightweight, ideology ridden and weak on general education.
(Professor Alan Smithers, University of Manchester)

Colleges suspect dirty tricks: schools break the law in their anxiety to persuade pupils not to go elsewhere. (College) brochures are dumped in corners and not distributed, careers teachers offer derisory information or sneer and deride colleges while discussing pupils' options (at post-16).
(From *Times Educational Supplement (TES)* report of research conducted for the Association of College Principals)

Hollow cries from the FE lobby: I think we in school sixth forms have heard more than enough whingeing from the further education lobby .... It is absurd to suggest that today's young people will not 'shop around' before settling on a place for the 16–19 period .... If colleges wonder why some students do not follow-up initial contacts, let them look to the chaos of their admissions procedures and registration arrangements for a start.
(Secondary headmaster's response to the above report)

The selection of quotations above gives a flavour of some of the current debates around 16–19 education. Few issues in education today are more controversial than those concerning the appropriate curricular, institutional and funding arrangements for 16–19 year olds in full-time education. In part this great interest can be explained by the fact that 16–19 education lies at the interfaces of compulsory schooling, further education, training, higher education and employment. As a result there is a proliferation of groups and individuals which can claim to have a legitimate interest in this phase of education. Scarcely a week goes by without an interest group or individual treating us to their views on 16–19 education in the educational or national press. Critics frequently refer to the 16–19 curriculum as a 'mess' or a 'jungle' despite the fact that one of the aims of the major reform of vocational qualifications undertaken in the 1980s with the introduction of the NVQ/GNVQ framework was to attempt to bring greater simplicity and coherence to the vocational curriculum. In response to criticisms of the 16–19 curriculum, in 1994 the government asked its favourite safe pair of hands Sir Ron Dearing 'to consider and advise the Secretaries of State for Education, Employment and Wales on ways to strengthen, consolidate and improve the framework of 16 to 19 qualifications' (Dearing, 1995). We shall make reference to the Dearing Review at appropriate points throughout the book.

But how do we explain the emergence of this vigorous debate at this particular time when throughout the 1950s, 1960s and into the 1970s 16–19 education cruised on, led by the flagship of A levels, with scarcely a ripple to disturb the calm? Much of the imperative for the reform of 16–19 education has its roots in the economic context. From the mid-1970s the education system has come under increasing pressure to meet the 'needs' of industry and commerce and play its part in reversing Britain's relative economic decline. Widespread youth unemployment in the late 1970s and through much of the 1980s only served to concentrate the minds of policy-makers on the 'problem' of the 16–19 curriculum. Particular emphasis was laid on the low levels of participation in post-compulsory full-time education and training, particularly in comparison with other developed countries. For example in 1986 the United Kingdom had the lowest full-time participation rate among 16–18 year olds of 13 Organisation for Economic Cooperation and Development (OECD) countries. The UK rate was 33 per cent, exactly half the average for the other 12 countries (Raffe, 1993b). This sort of evidence helped to create a broad consensus among policy-makers that a commonsense connection existed between the relative economic success of these countries and their much higher staying-on rates in post-compulsory education and that Britain's ailing economy was suffering due to our neglect of full-time education and training for 16–19 year olds.

A further and related pressure for increased participation and curriculum change has emanated from alleged changes in the nature of work, the labour market and organisational structures associated with the rise of post-fordism or flexible specialisation. The new forms of work organisation are characterised by changes in the nature of work processes, organisational structures and labour market operations. It has been suggested that workers will require greater flexibility, initiative and problem-solving abilities than were needed under fordism, with its armies of semi-skilled and unskilled machine operators and minders. Organisational hierarchies will become flatter, with the removal of tiers of supervisors and charge-hands making shop floor workers responsible for production and quality. Team working, the development of semi-autonomous work groups and quality circles are also claimed to be features of the new forms of work organisation. The aspiration of having a 'trade for life' is no longer appropriate. Workers must adapt to the prospect of regular changes of career. Even where a career nominally lasts a lifetime the actual nature of the work will be revolutionised. Flexibility is perhaps the key organising concept in post-fordism. Information technology and forms of computer control arc essential elements in facilitating this flexibility. All these changes have important implications for both the quantity and quality of the education and training offered to young people. For example the Employment Department report, *Labour Market and Skill Trends 1994-95*, states that not only will there be a 'long-term growth trend towards higher-skill white collar occupations' but that:

> It is becoming increasingly clear that the general skills content of most jobs is increasing. Jobs which are increasing in both numbers and skill levels will present the greatest challenge to the education and training system. Many of these are likely to be in skill-intensive knowledge based occupations.
>
> (DOE, 1993, p21)

The widespread belief that Britain is going to need a much more highly educated and trained workforce in the twenty-first century is reflected in the National Targets for Education and Training. Lifetime Learning Target 1 states that: By 2000, 60 per cent of young people by the age of 21 should achieve two A levels, an advanced GNVQ or an NVQ Level 3. This has clear implications for 16–19 education and training. Targets 2, 3 and 4 contain further ambitious goals related to the achievement of General Certificate of Secondary Education (GCSEs) at Grade C or above, intermediate GNVQs or NVQ Level 2 and achievements in core skills and the core subjects of the National Curriculum.

Of course, in the midst of all this human capital theory occasional dissenting voices have been raised arguing that there is no proven connection between education and training as a whole, let alone any particular age phases or types of curricula, and national economic prosperity. Other than at very high levels of generality, forecasts of the numbers and types of workers required in particular sectors have also been notoriously inaccurate and there appear to be no good reasons to believe that future forecasts will prove any more precise. In addition, empirical evidence for the existence and extent of post-fordist changes is both sparse and contentious. During the 1980s the United Kingdom labour market was marked by growth in employment in service industries, self employment and part-time employment (DOE, 1992) but there is limited evidence for a transformation in the nature of work (Grint, 1991). Grint argues plausibly, but speculatively, that elements of fordism, neo-fordism and post-fordism co-exist within the economy, within sectors and within enterprises. In similar vein Watkins has suggested that while there may be a growth of high tech *industries* there will be a preponderance of low tech *jobs* within these industries (Watkins, 1991).

However, the empirical justifications for these economic arguments for the expansion of 16–19 education and training need not detain us here, our purpose is to establish the powerful economic imperative which lies behind this growth. However, while the economic imperative is undoubtedly strong it is only one of several forces driving the expansion. Another is political, with all the main political parties agreed that expansion is a 'good thing' and vying with each other for the best ways of organising and funding it. There is also a social justice argument which supports the expansion as a means of helping young people fulfill their potential and open up a phase of education which until now has been, on this view, unacceptably élitist. Finally as we show in this book the expansion is being driven by 16–19 year olds themselves choosing in ever greater numbers to stay-on in full-time education, a development which has surprised many and raised serious funding issues. However, at the national policy-making level, human capital arguments hold sway. There is wide agreement across political parties, interest groups and among education professionals that increased participation in 16–19 education and training will have a significant pay-off in terms of national economic development and competitiveness (although the time-scale for such a pay-off remains uncertain).

Reform proposals

However, while there is a consensus that more education and training for 16 to 19 year olds would be a thoroughly good thing, there is far less agreement on its form and content. Richardson (Richardson, Woolhouse and Finegold, 1993) lists over 52 separate sets of recommendations for 16–19 reform over the two year period 1989–1991 and contrary to his expectation the publication of the White Paper *Education and Training for the 21st Century* (DES/DOE/Welsh Office, 1991) did not mark the end of the policy debate. The debate has not slackened and recent reports from the National Commission on Education and the Social Justice Commission have both made recommendations relevant to this area. The government's 1994 White Paper *Competitiveness: helping Business to Win* (DTI, 1994) also contained much of relevance to 16–19 education and training. In October 1994 six organisations representing heads and college principals in both the state and independent sectors issued a joint statement calling for major reform of 16–19 education and training (The Association for Colleges [AfC], the Girls' Schools Association [GSA], the Headmasters' Conference [HMC], the Secondary Heads' Association [SHA], the Sixth Form Colleges' Association [APVIC] and the Society of Headmasters and Headmistresses in Independent Schools [SHMIS], 1994) and as we write Sir Ron Dearing has outlined 'The Issues for Consideration' in his Review of 16–19 Qualifications. Given the longevity and wide-ranging nature of the debate which has been conducted it is not our intention to give a blow-by-blow account of the various contributions, instead in this opening chapter we aim to outline some of the main issues in the debates about appropriate curricular and institutional arrangements for the age group. Issues which are of specific relevance to particular elements of 16–19 education will be addressed in greater detail in the appropriate chapters.

The current system of 16–19 education and training is characterised by divisions between: academic and vocational courses; competence- and knowledge-based conceptions of learning; modular and non-modular curricula; continuous and terminal assessment; part-time and full-time study; schools and colleges; state and independent institutions. Whether these divisions promote healthy diversity or damaging divisiveness is at the heart of much of the argument about 16–19 education and training. Of course, dichotomies usually simplify matters and the divisions are not always so clear-cut as they may appear, but they do encapsulate radically different conceptions of 16–19 education and training.

There are two main views on the ways in which 16–19 education and training should be reformed. There are those who wish to maintain and improve the current multi-track system and those who propose a root and branch reform with replacement of the current curricular structures by a unified system. We now consider each of these positions in turn.

Reforming the multi-track system

The Conservative government, perhaps to its credit, has maintained a relatively clear and consistent line over a number of years. Its policy can be summarised as: (i) establishing three distinct curriculum tracks, and (ii) systematising and significantly strengthening the two vocational tracks while maintaining the traditional academic route.

The clearest expression of government policy was the 1991 White Paper *Education and Training for the 21st Century*. This set out plans to improve and develop the education and training system for 16 to 19 year olds. Nine overall aims were established, of which four are of particular relevance here. These were to:

> establish a framework of vocational qualifications that are widely recognised and used, and that are relevant to the needs of the economy;

> promote equal esteem for academic and vocational qualifications, and clearer and more accessible paths between them;

> extend the range of services offered by school sixth forms and colleges, so that young people face fewer restrictions about what education or training they choose and where to take it up;

> ensure that all young people get better information and guidance about the choices available to them at 16 and as they progress through further education and training.

> (DES/DOE/Welsh Office, 1991, p3)

Promoting vocational qualifications

Parts of the White Paper read like a panegyric to vocational qualifications. For example, it was asserted that vocational qualifications in this country have been undervalued and underused (p16). The White Paper then went on to outline the structure of NVQs and to pledge that their introduction would be speeded up. A highly significant element of the White Paper was the announcement of GNVQs for young people who want to study for vocational qualifications which prepare them for a range of related occupations but do not limit their choices too early as well as keeping open the possibility of moving on to higher education (p18). It was this announcement of the introduction of GNVQs which paved the way for the major changes in vocational courses in the schools which is the subject of Chapters 5 and 6 of this book. Another section of the White Paper, provocatively entitled 'Equal status for academic and vocational education', made a strong plea for equality of esteem. Young people's choices at 16, it was asserted, should not be limited by out-of-date distinctions between qualifications and institutions. The government wanted to remove the remaining barriers between the so-called academic and vocational routes. 'We want academic and vocational qualifications to be held in equal esteem' (p24). Within the White Paper this equal esteem was suggested by diagrams in which GCSE, A and Advanced Supplementary (AS) levels, GNVQs and NVQs were subsumed under the five level NVQ framework, which showed purported equivalencies between the different qualifications.

There was one section of the White Paper which suggested that the government was slightly more ambiguous about a multi-track system than other pronouncements indicated (the tantalising phrase 'so-called academic and vocational routes' also suggested that the authors of the White Paper considered the academic–vocational divide to be in some sense artificial). The White Paper contained a proposal to establish Ordinary and Advanced Diplomas. The Ordinary Diploma would be awarded to those achieving four or five good GCSEs while the Advanced Diploma would be for those achieving two or more A levels at grade C or above, equivalent vocational qualifications or a combination of the two. It was the notion that a course of study might combine or blend academic and vocational studies which would be contained within an umbrella qualification which was interesting. This seemed to run counter to the implicit assumption within much of the government's discourse on 16–19 education and training that there were three kinds of students for whom three distinct pathways would be created. Richardson (Richardson, Woolhouse and Finegold, 1993) argues that the proposal for the Advanced Diploma in the White Paper represented some seepage, at least at a rhetorical level, of the ideas of the reformers for the creation of a unified system into the Department for Education (DfE). However, since 1991 little has been heard about the Advanced Diploma. In a leaflet published in 1994 offering a brief guide to the three kinds of qualifications which can be studied for after the age of 16 the DfE makes no mention of the Advanced Diploma. The idea has been quietly left to die by the government although some interest groups have continued to promote the concept of an umbrella qualification embracing academic and vocational qualifications and the concept has recently re-emerged in Dearing's interim report (Dearing, 1995).

The period since 1991 has been distinguished by consistent efforts by the government to promote GNVQs and associate them more with academic qualifications than with NVQs. In July 1993 the then Secretary of State John Patten announced that Level 3 GNVQs would henceforth be known as Advanced GNVQs or vocational A levels. (In politically correct educational circles it sometimes became necessary to refer to GCE A levels and GNVQ A levels – not a practice which in our experience has won widespread acceptance). In December 1993 the Minister of Further and Higher Education Tim Boswell announced that with 70,000 students taking GNVQs, they were 'here to stay'. A month earlier the DfE had published a press release on the achievement of Katie Brown of Wootton Bassett School in Swindon in becoming the first student in the country to be awarded a vocational A level. Katie, we were told, had subsequently gone on to study at Bolton Institute of Higher Education. In August 1994 Secretary of State Gillian Shephard hailed the publication of GNVQ results as 'an historic step giving the country the vocational skills we need for the future' and congratulated the thousands of students who had completed the courses. If politicians' rhetoric could deliver parity of esteem for GNVQs they would surely have achieved it by now. Of course, it was not all plain sailing for the new qualifications, as we shall see in Chapter 6, but at this stage we only wish to establish that a major 'charm offensive' was launched by the government in pursuit of its policy of attaining parity of esteem for its new vocational qualifications.

The systematisation of vocational qualifications was achieved through the development of the NVQ framework. This currently has five levels, although as we write only Levels 1–3 are really operative. The intention of the reform was to establish clear and comparable standards and progression routes across the whole range of vocational qualifications. Over the last five years an increasing number of vocational qualifications have been revised and brought into this framework and in *Education and Training for the 21st Century* the government committed itself to accelerating this process. The essential features of NVQs are that they are competence-based, modular and intended to be workplace-based, although increasingly NVQ courses are being taken in colleges and in a much smaller number of schools. NVQs differ from GNVQs in being much more occupationally specific. This book is not centrally concerned with NVQs but it is important for the reader to keep in mind that they constitute the third track in the current system of 16–19 education and training. NVQs are important because the competence-based curriculum model developed for NVQs has influenced the development of GNVQs.

Reform of the academic track

In recent years there have been two main attempts to reform the academic track – the introduction of AS levels and the promotion of core skills. A brief analysis of each of these will be given here and taken up in more detail in the relevant chapters.

There has long been concern about what many see as the narrowness and over-specialisation of the standard three A level package. In the 1970s the Schools Council proposed the introduction of N and F levels as a means of addressing this perceived problem. (N levels were to be worth half an A level and F levels three-quarters and it was envisaged that the standard package for university entrance would be 3 N levels and 2 F levels). However, after considerable consultation and the carrying out of feasibility studies the suggestion came to nothing, mainly because the universities and examination boards were opposed to the proposals (Burchell, 1992). The next major proposal for the broadening of A levels was the report of the Higginson Committee in 1988 which advocated five, leaner A levels, only for the proposals to be rejected by the government on the day they were published. The government's approved method of broadening A level study has been the introduction and promotion of the AS level which is claimed to have half the content but all the rigour of a full A level. However, despite repeated attempts by the government to promote AS levels the take-up has been small and they have not achieved the prominence within the academic curriculum which was hoped for. Explanations for this relative failure will be explored in Chapter 4. The latest proposal, from Dearing, is for the development of AS levels as an intermediate qualification between GCSE and A level (Dearing, 1995).

A second attempt to reform the academic track was the core skills initiative of the late 1980s. Paul Coates in his review of this initiative attributes its origins to the then Secretary of State Kenneth Baker (Coates, 1991). This perhaps overlooks some of the support for core skills coming from teachers and other education professionals and their establishment as an integral part of vocational courses provided by City and Guilds, the Business and Technology Education Council (BTEC) and the Royal Society of Arts (RSA). Further impetus for the promotion of core skills was provided by the Technical and Vocational Education Initiative (TVEI). TVEI as a 14–18 project saw core skills as one means of enhancing progression across the 16+ divide and as a way of minimising the academic–vocational divide in the 16–19 curriculum. A more critical reading of the TVEI involvement would be that since the Initiative lacked the means to overcome the major structural divide in 16–19 education it was reduced to tinkering at the margins. Whatever the explanation, TVEI schemes encouraged a variety of strategies for identifying, promoting and implementing core skills in academic and vocational courses (Barnes et al., 1989). Following Baker's initiative a programme of research and consultation was instituted, mainly conducted by Her Majesty's Inspectorate of Schools (HMI), the National Curriculum Council (NCC) and the School Examinations and Assessment Council (SEAC). When the Education Secretary John McGregor commissioned reports from NCC and SEAC he described core skills as what 'all students need to be equipped to take their place in a modern economy as well as to be competent in every way to function in adult life generally'. As noted above the concept of core skills was familiar enough, not only from TVEI, but from vocational courses such as the Certificate of Pre-Vocational Education (CPVE) and BTEC, but as Coates says, the proposal that *all* students aged 16–19 should receive such core skills raised 'in a particularly sharp and urgent way, some fundamental questions which had always been attached to such core themes, or core skills, but which had not until then been exposed to detailed scrutiny' (Coates, 1991, p45). At the most fundamental level it raised the question of whether and to what extent core skills exist. For example, Coates (p47) discusses whether the concepts of problem-solving in history and in bricklaying have anything in common. The discussion about core skills sometimes exhibited a disturbing reductionism, not to say confusion, typical of many debates about 'skills', for example, in one of their contributions the CBI suggested 'integrity' as a core skill (CBI, 1989).

A full account of the often tortuous progress of the debate about core skills will be found in Chapter 7. It suffices here to note that after an initial flare of interest in the late 1980s rather less was heard about core skills as applied to the academic curriculum. On the other hand, core skills remain central to GNVQs although their role in NVQs is problematic. Some interest groups are strongly committed to the concept, the CBI for example see them as crucial to breadth and balance and to what they term 'careership' (CBI, 1993). Sir Ron Dearing was asked to consider whether we 'should encourage core skills, which are already an essential part of GNVQs, as part of the programmes of study for more 16 to 19 year olds?' In Chapter 7 we review the state of play in the core skills debate and draw on evidence for the core curriculum in the schools in which we conducted research.

One final point needs to be made concerning the reform of the academic curriculum. The apparent failure to bring about reform of the academic curriculum through AS levels and core skills should not lead us to conclude that A levels have not changed. There have been incremental changes in syllabuses, assessment patterns and methods, teaching and learning styles and a significant increase in modularisation. It might be that despite outward appearances A levels, or at least some of them, have changed significantly. We report the results of our research into these issues in Chapter 4.

David Raffe (Raffe, 1993a) in a penetrating analysis has summarised the arguments advanced in favour of multi-track systems. Among these probably the most widely heard argument in England and Wales is that it safeguards standards in the academic track and avoids adulterating the 'gold standard'. Interestingly, Raffe says that in other European countries another commonly advanced argument is that separate tracks safeguard standards in vocational courses by guarding against academic drift. It perhaps speaks volumes for the status of the vocational in England and Wales that this argument has rarely been put by the defenders of the current system. Another important argument for a multi-track system is that vocational courses prove motivating, especially for students averse to a 'rich academic diet' who prefer a more practical emphasis. Indeed further education colleges often claim to have succeeded in motivating students on vocational courses where the general education provided in schools pre-16 had failed.

Arguments for a unitary system

Arguments for a unified system of 16–19 education and training usually start with a critique of the existing arrangements. Richardson (Richardson, Woolhouse and Finegold, 1993) lists seven reports which recommended a move to a full unitary system and since his survey other influential reports have come out in favour of this option. The Institute of Public Policy Research report *A British Baccalaureate* (Finegold et al., 1990) still provides probably the most detailed specification of a unified system for England and Wales. The report asserts that reform of the different tracks is an inadequate response to the problem of 16–19 education and training and instead argues that these are part of a 'deeper malaise'. The report asserts that:

Britain's education system is marked by low 'staying-on' rates and poor comparative performance because it is divided. Most importantly, it divides 'academic' pupils from the rest through the different institutions, different curricula, different modes of study and above all different qualifications which cater for the two groups. Our qualifications system resembles an educational obstacle course and is designed to 'weed out' the majority of the pupils. We call this the early selection–low participation system.

(Finegold et al., 1990, p2)

In place of this divided system the IPPR proposed the creation of a unified system of qualifications at 16+. There would be a modular curriculum with core domains of social and human sciences; natural sciences and technology; arts, language and literature – with compulsory and optional modules within each domain. Each module would contain elements of academic and practical work. This structure, it was claimed, would avoid fragmentation and preserve breadth and 'reverse the debilitating divisions that currently exist between those selected to learn, those left to train and those for whom education and training end at 16' (p5). While the details of other schemes vary, the IPPR proposals embody the main characteristics of unified systems of 16–19 education and training. Raffe (Raffe, 1993a) suggests that the main strengths of unified systems are the ways in which they integrate academic and vocational studies, allow more individual and informal differentiation by making it possible to tailor courses of study to meet individual needs and allow incremental decision-making. However, he admits that there has been no evaluation of unified systems in action since only New Zealand has implemented anything approaching a comprehensive unified system, although weaker versions exist elsewhere. In the United Kingdom there has been increasing use of modular systems and credit accumulation and transfer in higher education, although even here there has only been a limited amount of evaluation of the effects of modularisation. There has also been some experience of modular systems in schools and colleges.

Having briefly reviewed some of the arguments in favour of multi-track and unified systems and introduced some of the more significant reform attempts and proposals, it is worth reiterating at this point that our sketches of both systems are to some extent ideal types. Many reform proposals have been aimed at making the multi-track system more flexible by allowing easier transfer and credit accumulation between different tracks (for example Kidd, 1991; CBI, 1993). Government policy has been moving somewhat in this direction although much more slowly than critics would wish. Judging from his Interim Report Sir Ron Dearing also appears to favour a more flexible multi-track system which would leave open the possibility of the development of a fully-fledged unified system in the future. The point is that in practice a highly flexible multi-track system may be virtually indistinguishable from a unitary system, the two ideal types exist on a continuum rather than in separate domains.

Contextual factors impinging on 16–19 education and training

Having reviewed some of the main dimensions of the debate about 16–19 education and training it is important to place this debate in the context of other changes taking place in education and training. There are three aspects of this context which will be briefly discussed here. The first two relate to changes in the curriculum of those phases of education which precede and succeed the 16–19 curriculum.

The effects of GCSE

At 14–16 the introduction of GCSE is widely held to have had a positive effect on staying-on rates at 16. In curriculum terms GCSE courses also introduced more student-centred methods with a greater emphasis on coursework (although coursework limitations were introduced in 1992) compared to many of the GCE courses which they replaced. The changed nature of the curricular experience 14–16 clearly raised important questions related to progression to both academic and vocational courses post-16 and there was a widespread feeling that either GCSE was an inadequate preparation for A level or that A level was a poor progression from GCSE. Although there is no evidence that GCSE has had an adverse effect upon A level examination results (Ashford, Gray and Tranmer, 1993) the perceived discontinuities between the two have acted as a pressure for change, although whether this should be upwards to A levels, downwards to GCSE or a combination of the two is a matter of controversy.

Changes in higher education

Changes have also taken place in higher education. The biggest of these has been the increased enrolment in higher education with 27.8 per cent of young people under 21 going on to full-time higher education in 1992. In the (slightly) longer term it appears that higher education in England and Wales is moving from an élite to a mass system and as this change proceeds it seems incontrovertible that it must impact on 16–19 education and training, although the specific nature of this impact remains unclear. Other important changes concern the development of modularisation and credit transfer in higher education and, as suggested above, this may provide an organisational model for 16–19 education. Within higher education there has also been increasing emphasis on independent and flexible learning techniques, partly as a response to increased enrolment. Empirical evidence on the extent of the use of these techniques in teaching and learning in higher education is lacking, but at a rhetorical level there is a perception of major changes in teaching and learning styles in higher education institutions.

In general then, changes whether real or perceived, in the organisational, curricular, pedagogical and assessment arrangements in both pre-16 and post-18 education have increased pressure for changes in 16–19 education and training, particularly with regard to A levels (see the quotation by Wagner at the opening of this chapter).

Changes in the organisation and funding of schools and colleges

Further contextual influences which have impacted on 16–19 education and training are measures related to the organisation and funding of schools and colleges. These were introduced as a result of the 1988 Education Reform Act and the 1992 Further and Higher Education Act. These acts introduced a more direct link between institutional funding and enrolment levels. Post-16 students are a particularly valuable commodity carrying funding of up to £3,000 per head. The 1988 Act also made it possible for schools to opt out of local authority control and become grant maintained. As a result of the 1992 Act all further education and sixth form colleges were removed from local authority control and became incorporated institutions funded directly by the Further Education Funding Council (FEFC). The combined effect of these changes was to greatly increase the competition between institutions for potential students, now unmediated to any extent by the LEAs. As is indicated in the final two quotations which begin this chapter this competition has generated considerable conflict in some localities.

A further consequence of recent changes has been that schools which did not have sixth forms were able to apply to the Secretary of State for permission to start one. For example, in February 1994 Secretary of State Patten announced the opening of eight new sixth forms, seven of which were at grant maintained schools. Critics claimed that these decisions were taken in an attempt to give grant maintained schools more status and encourage opting out. The county education officer for Hampshire, where three of the new sixth forms were situated, complained in the *TES* of 18 February 1994:

> The Secretary of State's concern about grant-maintained schools and their promotion has over-ridden the good educational and economic sense of the FEFC. (Both the FEFC and the LEA had objected to the establishment of the new sixth forms).

In the period February 1994 to September 1995 the Secretary of State for Education (later Education and Employment) approved 37 new sixth forms, 23 from grant maintained (GM) schools and 14 from local authority schools. Over the same period 33 proposals were rejected, 19 from GM schools and 14 from LEA schools. These figures show the strong tendency on the part of GM schools to apply to start sixth forms and while the Secretary of State has clearly shown some caution in granting proposals, almost two thirds of new sixth forms approved during this period have been in GM schools.

There is potential conflict between the government's policy of providing a diversity of competing institutional provision at post-16 and the dictates of efficient, cost-effective provision. A joint Audit Commission/Office for Standards in Education (OFSTED) report on full-time educational courses for 16–19 year olds (Audit Commission/OFSTED, 1993) showed that running costs per head for A level courses varied from £1,000 to £7,000 per year with smaller but still wide variations in costs for vocational courses. High costs were chiefly attributable to small teaching groups and the report suggested that if courses were organised so that there were no groups containing fewer than ten students costs could be cut very considerably. Clearly where costs are high sixth form provision is being subsidised from other elements of the school budget, although the report does not give details of precisely where these subsidies come from. The opening of new sixth forms seems likely to exacerbate problems of group size and efficiency. The Audit Commission was also strongly critical of the high drop-out and non-completion rates of post-16 courses and linked these to what it coyly called the 'bottoms on seats' incentives to recruit students to courses irrespective of their chances of success. The report suggested that local management of schools formulae should be modified to take account of rates of drop-out and unsuccessful course completion (however, more recent controversy over payment by outcomes for NVQ courses shows that this strategy is not without its problems).

The overall effect of recent legislation has been to strengthen institutional autonomy and heighten competition between institutions. It has now become virtually impossible for an LEA to introduce a tertiary scheme, in which all post-16 provision in a locality is concentrated in one institution with consequent economies of scale and potential for overcoming the academic–vocational divide. Provision of 16–19 education is now largely market-driven with little room for strategic planning by LEAs. However, in contrast to the managerial autonomy now enjoyed by schools and colleges considerable control over the curriculum is exercised by the Schools Curriculum and Assessment Authority (SCAA) and the National Council for Vocational Qualifications (NCVQ) through the restrictions which they are able to impose on the examining boards.

Increasing staying-on rates

Another important influence on the sixth form curriculum has been the quite remarkable increases in staying-on rates, particularly since 1987/88. Figure 1.1 shows increases in the percentages of 16 year olds in England staying in full-time education over the period 1983/84 to 1993/94.

The actual numbers of full-time students have been increasing since 1988/89 and the estimated figures for 1994/95 stood at an all time high of 393,500. Participation rates by 17 and 18 year olds in full-time education have also been increasing, for 17 year olds from 35.2 per cent in 1983/84 to 58.6 per cent in 1994/95 and for 18 year olds from 16.6 per cent in 1983/84 to 38.4 per cent in 1994/95. For 16 and 17 year olds a higher percentage of females than males have stayed on in each of the

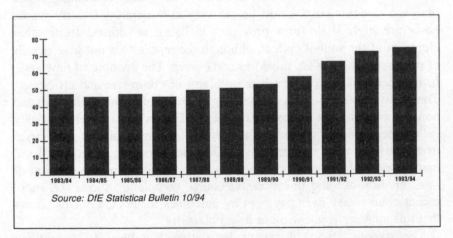

Source: DfE Statistical Bulletin 10/94

Figure 1.1 % participation of 16 year olds in full-time education 1983/84 to 1993/94

eleven years. For 18 year olds during the period 1983/84 to 1988/89 a higher percentage of males were still in full-time education but from 1989/90 the percentage of females has been higher in this age group also.

Over the same period there have been significant decreases in each of the three age groups in the percentages of part-time students. For 16 year olds there has been a decline from a high of 18.4 per cent in 1988/89 to 7.7 per cent in 1994/95. Clearly there has been a shift from part-time to full-time study among 16 year olds. However, there has also been an increase in the percentages involved in part-time and full-time education from 64.3 per cent in 1983/84 to 80 per cent in 1993/94.

The data for all three age groups and for males and females show a consistent pattern in which staying-on rates remained fairly stable in the period 1983–1987/88 (even registering a small decline in 1986/87), but from 1988/89 there have been strong and consistent increases, for 16 year olds of 21.2 per cent over a five year period. It may be that this great increase in staying-on in full-time education at 16-19, particularly when coupled with the expansion of higher education, will prove to be one of the most significant social changes of the 1980s and 1990s. However, estimated figures for staying-on rates for 1994–95 suggest that for the first time for almost a decade there has been a slight reduction in staying-on rates for 16 year olds and a slowing rate of increase for staying-on at 17 and 18. If these data are confirmed it would appear consistent with full-time staying-on rates at 16 reaching a plateau at around 70 per cent.

The reasons for the increases in staying-on rates remain, to some extent, mysterious and have confounded many of the analyses of the low participation rates pre-1988. The IPPR report, for example, asserted that the divided nature of 16–19 education and training was a cause of low participation (Finegold et al., 1990), but the success of the divided system in generating much higher staying-on rates has challenged this assertion (of course it could be argued that staying-on rates in England are still below those of competing countries and that the rate of increase is showing signs of slackening off, halting or even going into reverse, in which case it might be premature to assume that the 'problem' of low participation has been solved). As we shall see in Chapters 2 and 7 a commonly held view among students and teachers in the schools was that the recession of the late 1980s and early 1990s, coupled with changes in the benefit regulations for 16 year olds, were chiefly responsible for the increased staying-on rates. This is likely to be part of the explanation, but in the early 1980s youth labour market conditions were roughly comparable to those in the late 1980s and early 1990s and yet the staying-on rates remained stubbornly low.

Thus, over a ten year period the reactions of 16 year olds to similar labour market conditions changed markedly. One significant change has been that large numbers of 16 year olds who in the first half of the 1980s would have left school and entered the Youth Training Scheme and its successor Youth Training (YT) are now staying-on in full-time education. Thus, whatever the attractions of YT or the disincentives of full-time education may have been a decade ago the perceptions of a significant number of young people in the 1990s have changed and the balance of perceived benefits has swung strongly in favour of staying in full-time education.

The rise in staying-on rates is also commonly associated with the introduction of GCSE. The consistent improvements in grades over the life of GCSE have meant that more young people have considered themselves qualified to stay-on. Many schools require 4 or 5 GCSEs at grades A–C for entry to Advanced level courses, although as we shall see these requirements are more likely to be strictly adhered to for A levels than for GNVQs. Thus the rising proportions of 16 year olds gaining these qualifications partly explains the increase in A level entries. However, the Youth Cohort Study (YCS) (Ashford, Gray and Tranmer, 1993) also found significant increases in staying-on amongst students with poorer grades. Indeed one of the remarkable features of the YCS data was the consistent nature of the increases in staying-on rates across gender, ethnic and family and parental circumstances (p4). Ashford, Gray and Tranmer (1993) suggest that among other factors such as the expansion of higher education, the introduction of new courses and qualifications post-16 and changes in the youth labour market and benefit regulations, the GCSE effect 'may well have been amongst the most important at this time' (p12).

However, the national figures on staying-on rates hide wide variations across LEAs. Taking the figures for 16 year olds by full-time participation rate the lowest staying-on rate in 1992/93 among English LEAs was 49 per cent, the highest 87 per cent. There were marked regional variations. Of the fifteen LEAs with staying-on rates of lower than 60 per cent all but one were northern authorities (the exception was Sandwell in the West Midlands). The ten authorities with staying-on rates in excess of 80 per cent were all in the south-east and of the 29 authorities with the highest staying-on rate only three were in the north and two in the Midlands. Data collected in West and North Yorkshire also show that there are variations in staying-on rates between schools in the same LEA.

It is likely that much of the variation can be partially explained by socio-economic factors. However, there seem to be other local factors at work because there are wide variations in the rate of increase in staying-on between authorities with roughly similar socio-economic conditions. In Inner London, for example, staying-on increased by 24 per cent between 1988/89 and 1992/93 but for metropolitan authorities the rate of increase was 16 per cent. Within metropolitan authorities there were wide variations with Rochdale recording a 6 per cent increase and Coventry a 24 per cent increase.

We turn now to participation by courses and institutions over the period 1983/84 to 1993/94.

Figure 1.2 shows changes in the main courses studied by students who stay-on in full-time education. There are four features of the statistics which deserve to be highlighted. First, there has been a marked increase in the percentages of students studying A/AS levels (from 21.7 per cent in 1983/84 to 36.7 per cent in 1993/94). Second, the percentages taking

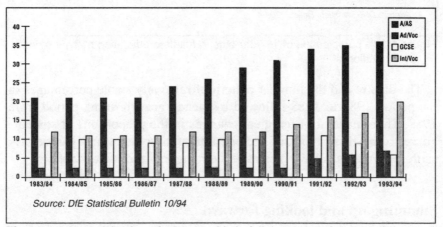

Source: DfE Statistical Bulletin 10/94

Figure 1.2 % participation of 16 year olds in full-time education by main course

intermediate and foundation level vocational qualifications, e.g. CPVE, Diploma of Vocational Education (DVE), BTEC First, GNVQ Intermediate, have also risen rapidly since 1990/91. Third, Advanced level vocational courses, e.g. BTEC National, GNVQ Advanced, show a slower rate of increase. Fourth, GCSE entries have fluctuated over the 11 year period but have shown a clear decline since 1991/92.

It can be seen that while the balance between A/AS levels and non-A/AS levels has remained largely stable, among those not taking A/AS levels there has been a decline in GCSE re-sits and an increase in both Intermediate and Advanced level vocational courses.

Figure 1.3 shows the breakdowns for attendance by 16 year olds participating in full-time education by schools, sixth form colleges and tertiary/further education colleges.

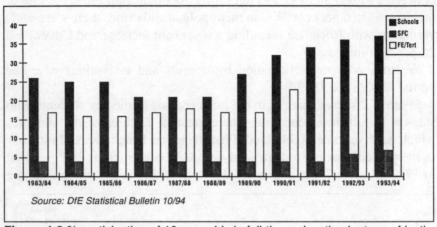

Source: DfE Statistical Bulletin 10/94

Figure 1.3 % participation of 16 year olds in full-time education by type of institution

The data reveal the familiar pattern of relatively stable percentages in the period 1983 to 1988 followed by steady growth in the period from 1988. There have not been great changes in the proportions of students going to the three types of sectors, although colleges and particularly sixth form colleges have increased their share of the student cohort.

Summing up and looking forward

This chapter has set the scene for the remainder of the book by providing an overview of 16–19 education and some of the issues which are currently matters of considerable debate. As we write 16–19 education is buoyant and expansive, students are flooding in as never before and while there are inevitable problems and frustrations, the 16–19 phase has at least avoided some of the worst effects of the curriculum and assessment planning blight which have affected the 5–16 curriculum. Schools, colleges and teachers can legitimately feel that as students are voting so positively with their feet they must be doing something right. The government too can always counter criticism of its policy on 16–19 education by pointing to the dramatic improvements in staying-on rates. There is no room for complacency, however, since we cannot be sure if 16 year olds are staying-on because of the attractions of full-time education, the unattractiveness of the alternatives or both. Also while it is true that staying-on rates in England and Wales are much higher than they were, they are still below those in many comparable countries. A large proportion of those who stay-on at 16 also do so for only one year. Thus overall staying-on rates for the 16–19 age group are arguably still below the levels required for a modern twenty-first century economy.

Certainly the debate goes on between those who favour the existing multi-track system and those who want radical reform and the establishment of a unitary, modular system comprising academic and vocational elements for all. Of course, many individuals and groups take a more moderate position seeking reforms which will bring greater breadth, flexibility and transferability to the system.

Much of the remainder of this book comes down from the rarefied air of policy-making and system-building which has been the subject of much of this opening chapter. The 16–19 debate is well populated with policy-makers, system-builders, commentators and critics who have debated the virtues and shortcomings of a wide variety of approaches. We intend this book to be firmly anchored in a description and analysis of the ways in which schools, teachers and students are actually making sense of the dynamic and contentious climate in which they find themselves while locating this practice in relation to wider issues within the 16–19 debate.

CHAPTER 2

An Overview of the 16–19 Curriculum

This chapter will provide an overview of the sixth form curriculum based on questionnaire data from schools in West and North Yorkshire and upon national data where appropriate. Our intention is to provide an overall picture of the school sixth form which will assist readers in locating the more detailed descriptions and analyses of the constituent elements of the curriculum in the following chapters. This chapter will address the following issues: staying-on rates, size of sixth forms, enrolments for academic and vocational courses, core curricular provisions and recent and planned changes in sixth form curricula. However, before proceeding to detailed consideration of these elements we present a case study of curriculum provision in one school. This school (the name is fictitious) has a large and thriving sixth form and thus gives an indication of the provision which may be found, although as we shall show there are considerable variations between schools.

CASE STUDY: Manor Park School

Manor Park School has 1,700 students on roll with a sixth form of almost 250. The school is situated in a rural area, but faces competition for students from two nearby further education colleges. Two slightly more distant selective schools also cream off some students of high academic ability at age 11. Thus although the school does not face the cut-throat competition for students at 16+ which affects many urban schools, neither does it enjoy any sort of local monopoly of 16+ provision and there is competition among schools and colleges in the area to recruit students at 16+. The school provides a comprehensive sixth form curriculum and has a long history of involvement in vocational education. Senior staff are well informed and forward-looking, the sixth form is expansive and buoyant and examination results at GCSE and A level are above both national and LEA averages. This school therefore presents a positive and self-confident response to the national and local contexts within which the sixth form curriculum is constructed.

The courses offered in 1994/95 were as follows.

Table 2.1 Advanced Courses

A Level		GNVQ
Art	Pure Mathematics & Mechanics	Business
Biology	Pure Mathematics & Statistics	Design
Business Studies	Music	Science
Chemistry	Philosophy & Theology	
Classical Civilisation*	Physics	
Economics	Psychology	
English Language	Russian*	
English Literature	Sociology	
French	Statistics**	
Geography	Technology*	
Geology	Theatre Studies	
German*		
History		
Pure Mathematics*		

*AS available as well as A level   **AS level only*

Table 2.2 Intermediate Courses

GNVQ	GCSE MATURE	BTEC FIRST
Business	Art	Information Technology
Design	English	
Health & Social Care	Environmental Science	
	Language	
	Mathematics	
	Media Studies	
	Science	
	Sociology	
	Technology	

This curriculum provision invites several comments. A level provision is extensive, although not all the subjects offered may run. However, in 1992/93 twenty-seven subjects were examined at A level. Group sizes varied considerably, the largest examination entries (excluding General Studies) were in Chemistry (24 entries), English Language (23), Geography (23), Maths Pure/Applied (23),

Physics (21). In contrast nine subjects (Applied Maths, Computer Science, German, Geology, Pure Maths, Music, Religious Education, Russian and Theatre Studies) had five or fewer entries. The Audit Commission recommendation that courses should not run with fewer than ten students has clear relevance here. The second general observation concerns the relatively large number of AS subjects on offer. However, evidence from earlier years suggested that few, if any, of the AS level courses would recruit students and where they did run they would be taught together with A level students (an almost universal practice in AS level provision). The school was unusual in continuing to offer a relatively large range of GCSE courses, although this was reduced from that taken in 1992/93 when 20 GCSE subjects were taken by Year 12 students. On the vocational side the school offered a substantial package with three GNVQ courses at both Advanced and Intermediate levels. The school had also rapidly shifted from BTEC to GNVQ, while retaining a BTEC First course in an area where the replacement GNVQ course was yet to come on stream. The school was quick to adopt GNVQ Advanced Science in its first post-pilot year and was one of relatively few schools to offer GNVQ Art & Design at both Intermediate and Advanced levels. Of particular interest is the way in which the sixth form prospectus promoted the parity of academic and vocational courses. This was done both by displaying the courses side by side in tabular form as shown above and through the advice which was offered to students in the prospectus. For example, those who had obtained four or five GCSE grades C or higher were advised that:

'You are ready for Advanced level study and must now decide whether you wish to study a course of three A levels or mix A levels with one or two AS levels or whether you wish to choose a GNVQ Advanced Course'.

A flow chart which was included in the prospectus further emphasised that the essential distinction in the sixth form curriculum was between Intermediate and Advanced levels rather than academic and vocational courses. The presentation of the courses in this way also encouraged combinations of academic and vocational courses and on our visit to the school we met students who were combining an A level with a GNVQ Advanced course. In sum, there was a deliberate and determined attempt on the part of senior managers to promote parity of esteem between vocational and academic routes through the sixth form prospectus and other documents provided to students and their parents. Of course, as the deputy head acknowledged, the establishment of parity of esteem in these ways in school documents did not ensure that this was reflected in the individual and often informal counselling provided by staff to students and parents. However, our rather limited evidence suggests that there were students taking GNVQ Advanced courses who could have taken A levels and this contrasted with the situation in many other schools both in our study and nationally (FEU, Institute of Education and Nuffield Foundation, 1994).

The prospectus gave little emphasis to the extra-main course curriculum. A single page towards the end of the booklet referred to the 'Core Entitlement' package available in Year 12. This emphasised 'Information Technology and Communications', stated that a modern foreign language can be studied 'if desired' and also mentioned Economic & Industrial Awareness and Personal & Social Issues. There was reference to pastoral support and action planning. It was stated that General Studies was available at both A level and GCSE as a progression from the Core Entitlement. The largest section was devoted to outlining the careers/higher education guidance available in the sixth form. As we show in Chapter 7 the low profile of the core curriculum in the documentation reflected the curricular reality in this school and most others.

Having given a flavour of the character of the school sixth form in the 1990s we now turn to a more general analysis of the curriculum and examine first the patterns of staying-on in the schools which were included in our research.

Staying-on in the sixth form

Chapter 1 established the pattern of considerable increases in staying-on rates during the second half of the 1980s. This was reflected in the six LEAs in which our research was based.

Table 2.3 illustrates that while the figures broadly correspond to the national data in showing increases in staying-on there are some interesting local variations. Leeds alone recorded an increase greater than the average for England and in this was unusual among LEAs throughout northern England. Calderdale and Wakefield were unusual in registering declines in staying-on in some years. There are indications from Bradford, Calderdale and Leeds that staying-on rates are beginning to stabilise and the most recent national figures have also tended to confirm

Table 2.3 % full-time participation rates for 16 year olds in North and West
Yorkshire

	88/89	89/90	90/91	91/92	92/93	Change 88–93
Bradford	45	50	52	59	59	14
Calderdale	53	64	63	66	65	12
Kirklees	54	56	57	63	68	14
Leeds	42	46	53	61	62	20
Wakefield	52	55	53	59	65	13
North Yorks	58	61	66	69	72	14
England	51	55	59	67	70	19

Source: DfE Statistical Bulletin 11/94

this. Interpretation of the data is fraught with difficulties. While some
variations, such as the differences between staying-on rates in Bradford
compared to North Yorkshire, can be confidently accounted for partly in
terms of socio-economic factors, the reasons for other variations between
LEAs and over time remain mysterious.

Turning to school level staying-on data further wide variations were
discovered, often within LEAs. Within both Bradford and Leeds, for
example, there were schools which had full-time staying-on rates at 16+
(both in the schools and in other institutions) of below 50 per cent and
other schools which had rates in excess of 80 per cent. Figure 2.1 shows
the staying-on rates at schools responding to our questionnaire.

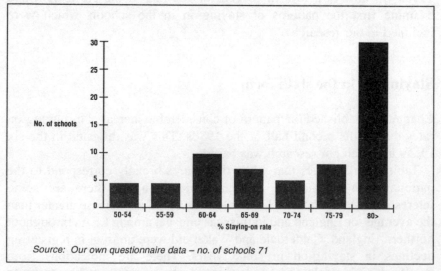

Source: Our own questionnaire data – no. of schools 71

Figure 2.1 Staying-on rate at 16 at schools in North and West Yorkshire in
1993–94

The number of schools with staying-on rates in excess of 80 per cent is swelled by the inclusion of each of the 12 independent schools which responded to the questionnaire and by seven North Yorkshire schools. Staying-on rates for North Yorkshire schools were generally towards the upper end of the scale with no school having a rate of lower than 60 per cent. Other LEA and grant maintained schools were spread more evenly.

The questionnaire asked schools to estimate the percentages of students in Year 11 in 1992/93 staying-on in full-time education both in that school and elsewhere. In general far more students chose to remain at the same school where they had taken their GCSEs than to move elsewhere and in Chapter 8 we examine the reasons which students gave for preferring to remain where they were. As already indicated in Chapter 1 there have been allegations from colleges of schools pulling 'dirty tricks' in order to retain students at 16+. However, there were wide variations in the percentages of students switching from the schools to another provider of full-time post-16 education. (We do not have information on which institutions these students went to, but from our interview data all the indications are that most of those who left state schools went to colleges. We met few students who moved from one state school with a sixth form to another. However, there does seem to be some evidence that some students move from independent schools to state school sixth forms.) In some schools (12 out of 70) fewer than one in ten students left to pursue full-time education elsewhere, while at the other end of the scale in 21 schools more than one in four students changed institutions. In one North Yorkshire school as many students left to pursue their education elsewhere as remained in the school. Few patterns are discernible in the data. For example, comparing two rather similar schools in Leeds, in one only 2 per cent of the cohort left to pursue full-time education elsewhere, whereas in the other the figure was 26 per cent. Similar contrasts could be drawn in other LEAs. There appear to be no obvious local factors or major differences in sixth form curricular provision which could account for these variations, so we presume that they must be explicable in terms of in-school processes and characteristics, although what these were remains uncertain. Another general feature of the data was the seepage of students from independent schools into the state system at 16+. Two independent schools were losing over one third of their cohort and in most others there was a loss of between 10 per cent and 25 per cent of the cohort, although it was also notable that the most prestigious schools tended to keep most of their students at 16+.

This brief discussion of staying-on rates in North and West Yorkshire has revealed a number of interesting variations while confirming in general terms the national patterns illustrated in Chapter 1. It is evident that there are complex local and institutional causal processes at work which are not well understood in the local authorities and schools themselves and which lead to considerable variations in the responses of young people to the choices facing them at 16. Despite these complex and somewhat baffling variations however, some generalisations can be safely made. The most obvious is that we have been in an era of expansion of the sixth form. More students have been staying-on at school and this opened-up all sorts of possibilities and imperatives for curriculum reform and development. The most recent data on staying-on rates suggests that the period of expansion may be coming to an end with staying-on rates at 16 stabilising at around 70 per cent. The case study which began this chapter indicated some of the ways in which schools have sought to develop their sixth forms and much of the rest of the book explores in greater detail ways in which the schools are responding to the context in which they find themselves.

The size of the sixth form

The optimum size of the sixth form has been a matter of some debate. Sir Christopher Ball, a ubiquitous commentator on the 16–19 curriculum, argued in the TES that a sixth form should have 'not less than 400 and possibly as high as 500' students. The 'obvious long-term solution' in his view was to create 'a tertiary sector of sixth form and FE colleges'. He recognised that a lower limit of 500 would close most existing sixth forms but suggested that as a modest first step schools should be given three years in which to bring their sixth forms up to 250 after which any school which failed to meet that target would be denied the freedom to run sixth forms (TES, 4 November 1994). Two weeks later in the TES (18 November) the Chief Education Officer of Staffordshire challenged Ball's sums and argued that for a school offering 15 A levels and five GNVQs the 'critical mass' for a sixth form would be 200, with a considerably lower figure where the school was collaborating with other providers as, he claimed, was the case with 'most institutions'.

How did the size of sixth forms in the schools included in our study match up to these prescriptions? The average sizes were as shown in Table 2.4, and Figure 2.2 shows the distribution of the size of sixth forms in North and West Yorkshire.

Table 2.4 Average size of sixth forms in North and West Yorkshire schools
1993–94

Bradford	176
Leeds	121
Kirklees	161
Calderdale	129
Wakefield	176
North Yorks	159
GM	162
Independent	167
ALL	152

Source: School Performance Tables 1994

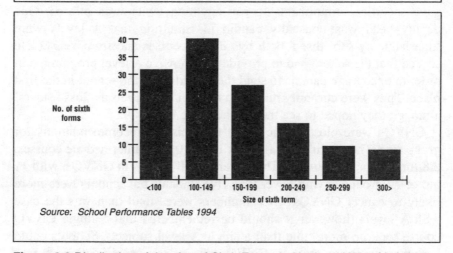

Source: School Performance Tables 1994

Figure 2.2 Distribution of the size of Sixth Forms in North and West Yorkshire
schools 1993–94

Thus even if we take the more conservative estimate of 200 as the critical mass for a sixth form 77 per cent of the sixth forms in North and West Yorkshire were smaller than this. We do not have detailed information on the number of schools which were collaborating with other post-16 providers but we suggest that 'most' is a considerable over-estimate and often where collaboration was taking place it was on a small scale. Overall there is no doubt that there were a large number of small sixth forms in the schools and small sixth forms invariably mean small teaching groups in some subjects. We did not collect systematic data on the size of A level groups but the situation described in the case study school at the start of this chapter was very common. Subjects such as Art,

Music, Theatre Studies, Computer Studies and some modern languages frequently ran with small groups. Of course, from a pedagogical viewpoint there may be much to be said in favour of small teaching groups, provided they are not too small, but as the Audit Commission pointed out, these small groups were being subsidised from elsewhere within the school budget, either from within the sixth form or more likely from Key Stages 3 or 4. Again this may be justified, but in the schools that we visited few attempts were made to justify it. Indeed, while school managers were aware in general terms of the costs of small sixth form teaching groups few schools had attempted to quantify these costs and justify them against other priorities. Rather a sort of inertia seemed to be operating where because subjects had always been offered at A level they tended to continue to be offered unless a specific event such as the departure of a member of staff brought about a reappraisal. Some schools gave specific commitments to run anything which was offered. One deputy head was unusually candid in admitting that A levels were 'unashamedly subsidised' both by GNVQ courses and from Year 9. He argued that the school had to provide an extensive A level programme in order to encourage parents to send their children to the school in the first place. They were currently running a number of A levels as 'loss leaders' although they hoped to see the numbers rise.

GNVQs were close to the Audit Commission recommendations for group size. The overall average was 10.1 (10.6 for Intermediate courses, 8.8 for Advanced courses). There were small groups in GNVQs, with 11 out of 77 groups having fewer than five students but schools were more likely to cancel GNVQs when numbers were small than was the case with A levels (however it should be remembered that a single GNVQ course took up more time than a single A level subject). Schools could legitimately argue that as GNVQ was a new qualification it was reasonable to support small groups in the first year or two while the courses became established and indeed demand did appear to be building for GNVQs both in the schools we studied and nationally.

The issue of the size of sixth forms and of teaching groups within them remains important. In the context of the quasi-education market created by recent legislation, decisions about the size of sixth forms and teaching groups are largely in the hands of schools. No-one has the power to tell headteachers and governing bodies which courses should or should not run, let alone whether they should or should not have a sixth form where one already exists. Indeed as we noted in Chapter 1 the trend is clearly in favour of more school sixth forms opening. We do not want to suggest that there is necessarily anything wrong with the subsidisation of sixth forms in general or of particular subjects within the curriculum. However, we do suggest that where such subsidisation is taking place it should be quantified, made transparent and justified against other priorities. Our research suggests that either deliberately as a matter of managerial policy or more likely through default, this happens rarely in schools at present.

The sixth form curriculum

This book is primarily about the sixth form curriculum and in the chapters that follow we dissect that curriculum in some detail. Our purpose here is to place the more qualitative analysis which follows into a quantitative framework derived from our questionnaire returns and nationally available statistics.

As we saw in Chapter 1 the 16–19 curriculum can be largely thought of in terms of three tracks – the academic and the two vocational tracks (GNVQ and NVQ). The NVQ track is largely absent from school sixth forms and in the past the other two tracks (to the extent to which the vocational track has existed at all in some schools) have been largely separate with students opting for one or the other. While there is disagreement among national policy-makers over the desirability of maintaining separate tracks there is more consensus on making possible the combination of elements from different tracks and even the government, which has generally favoured a somewhat purist approach, acknowledged the possibility of blending academic and vocational qualifications in the White Paper, *Education and Training for the 21st Century* (DES/DOE/Welsh Office, 1991).

In order to discover the extent to which this sort of blending was already taking place we asked schools to indicate which combinations of courses, if any, students were following. The results are shown in Figure 2.3

It is evident that combinations of advanced level courses, i.e. a GNVQ Advanced course + one A level or one or two AS levels were rarities. Indeed over half the occurrences of combinations of A/AS levels and vocational courses are accounted for by two schools in which all A level students, except those taking four A levels, were enrolled in the Diploma of Vocational Education, an arrangement which seems unlikely to be extended to GNVQ courses as the DVE is phased out. Predictably 38 per cent of students taking vocational courses are also taking, or more likely re-taking GCSEs. Typically students who entered GNVQ courses, particularly at Intermediate level, had achieved a mixed bag of grades at

32

GCSE and many re-took English and Maths in an attempt to attain grade C or better. Twelve per cent of A level candidates were also taking GCSEs, many of these were also re-takes although some may have been new subjects taken as part of a core or supplementary studies programme. The essential point to emerge from the data is that the two tracks available in schools remained very much separate with students opting for one or the other.

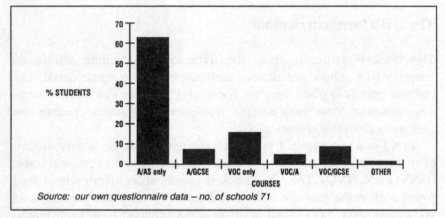

Source: our own questionnaire data – no. of schools 71

Figure 2.3 Course combinations in North and West Yorkshire schools 1993–94

Having established that the separate tracks remain relatively insulated from each other in schools' sixth forms we now turn to the distribution of students between the tracks. This is shown in Figure 2.4.

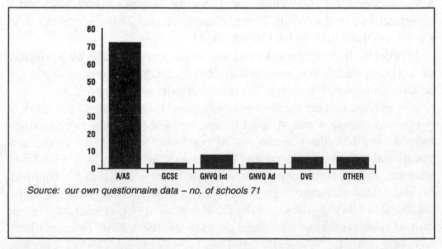

Source: our own questionnaire data – no. of schools 71

Figure 2.4 Year 12 students by main courses in North and West Yorkshire schools 1993–94

The school sixth form continues to be dominated by A levels with three out of every four students taking them as their main course. Vocational courses were in a transitional phase at the time the questionnaires were administered as the DVE and other vocational courses (largely BTEC First and National Diplomas) were being phased out and replaced by GNVQs. Aggregating vocational courses, 23 per cent of students were taking them as their main course. However the inclusion of independent schools does have an important impact on the figures. Of over 1,000 students surveyed in independent schools not a single one was taking a vocational course and only four were taking GCSEs. The independent school sixth form curriculum remained totally dominated by A levels and none of the schools had any immediate plans to introduce GNVQs. Thus, excluding independent schools, in state schools the breakdown of students by main courses was 69 per cent A/AS levels, 3 per cent GCSE, 28 per cent vocational courses.

The second year sixth (Year 13) was everywhere dominated by A/AS levels which account for 94 per cent of all students. The remaining students were mainly enrolled on GNVQ Advanced or BTEC National courses. We would expect enrolments in GNVQ Advanced courses to increase, but this may be a slow process in the schools as in Year 12 only 3 per cent of students were enrolled in these courses. National figures suggest that more than half of 16 year olds who stay on in full-time education do so for only one year. There was evidence of the emergence of a three year sixth form course comprising GNVQ Intermediate followed by GNVQ Advanced course although at the time of our study this was still on a very small scale.

The academic curriculum

Having established the continued importance of academic courses within the sixth form curriculum we now turn to a brief consideration of A and AS level courses. The academic curriculum is examined in much greater detail in Chapters 3 and 4 and our intention here is merely to outline some of the main general trends.

The number of A level candidates has increased gradually over the last three years from 649,669 in 1991 to 734,623 in 1993, a 13 per cent increase. This increase in candidates has reflected the general increases in staying-on rates noted in Chapter 1. Another noteworthy feature of A levels are the large number of syllabuses. In 1994 there were over 410 divided among the eight examination boards and although this represents a slight reduction in the total number there is no evidence of the sort of major rationalisation which took place at GCSE level.

The distribution of A level candidates between subjects is shown by Figure 2.5.

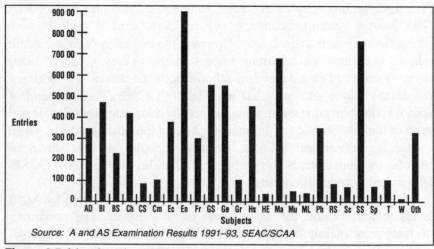

Source: A and AS Examination Results 1991–93, SEAC/SCAA

Figure 2.5 A level entries 1994

Abbreviations: AD – Art and Design; BI – Biology; BS – Business Studies; Ch – Chemistry; CS – Computer Studies; Cm – Communication Studies; Ec – Economics; En – English; Fr – French; GS – General Studies; Ge – Geography; Gr – German; Hs – History; HE – Home Economics; Ma – Maths; Mu – Music; ML – Modern Languages; Ph – Physics; RS – Religious Studies; Sc – Science; SS – Social Science; Sp – Spanish; T – Technology; W – Welsh; Oth – All other subjects

Figure 2.6 shows percentage changes in subject entries 1991–93.

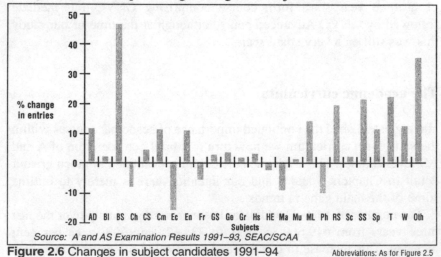

Source: A and AS Examination Results 1991–93, SEAC/SCAA

Figure 2.6 Changes in subject candidates 1991–94   Abbreviations: As for Figure 2.5

These data show some important trends. Of course percentage increases disguise the fact that some of these subjects are starting from low bases so that relatively small increases in candidate numbers produce large percentage increases. For example an increase of 700 candidates represents an 18.5 per cent increase in Modern Language candidates (excluding French, German and Spanish). Similarly the spectacular increase in Business Studies entries is from a relatively low base. However, the data does suggest that there has been a shift from Economics to Business Studies courses and this reflects, and is perhaps a consequence of, similar changes taking place at GCSE level (see Williams and Yeomans, 1994). Of greater significance because larger numbers of candidates are involved is the decline in entries in Maths, Physics and Chemistry, at a time when A level entries as a whole are increasing. The third main science subject, Biology, has managed to increase its numbers slightly, although by less than the average for A levels as a whole. Whereas it is plausible to speculate that students who are not taking the other three subjects which registered declines, Economics, Home Economics or French, are instead taking Business Studies, Technology or Spanish, it seems likely that candidates who in other years might have taken Physics, Chemistry and Maths are being lost to science and maths (these entry figures are prior to the introduction of GNVQ Science and it remains to be seen what effects, if any, this will have on A level science entries). French and German also have not done particularly well, failing to reflect the overall increase in A level entries. In contrast the arts and humanities subjects have been buoyant. The more traditional subjects, Art and Design, History and Geography have shown steady increases, English has grown powerfully from an already high base and strong gains have been made by Sociology, Psychology, Law, Media Studies, Theatre Studies and Sports Studies. The overall picture is of a steady and clearly identifiable trend away from the sciences and towards the arts, humanities and social sciences in the A level curriculum.

On the face of it this trend might be seen as unfortunate by those who promote the expansion of 16–19 education and training on economic grounds, since it is a common view that maths and science are greater promoters of national economic regeneration than, for example, sociology, law and theatre studies. Set against this, however, is the growth in subjects such as business studies and technology which are often claimed to have a strong connection with economic growth. This drift away from mathematics and the sciences and towards what critics call 'soft' subjects has been taken by some as evidence of a decline in A level standards. The economic argument founders on the fact that we know little about the effects of subjects studied at A level on the subsequent economic 'productivity' of individuals. It has often been argued that generic abilities claimed to be promoted by A level courses are of greater importance than any specific knowledge and skills developed through particular subjects and that therefore trends in subject choice are not important. Nor do we have any basis for judging how many maths, science and modern language students are 'needed' at A level in order to satisfy economic imperatives. The main point to be made here is that the choices of young people do not respond to generalised rhetoric about the 'national good' requiring more students to study maths and science. It has been argued that the drift to the arts, humanities and social sciences represents a rational response to labour market conditions by young people (Chapman, 1991). We suspect that many of the policy-makers who have urged the expansion of 16–19 education and training would not have wished to see more students studying sociology or media studies but young people have their own reasons for choosing to pursue particular subjects. The argument that some of the subjects which have shown growth, such as Media Studies and Sports Studies are 'soft' options is difficult to address. Research by Newcastle University's A level Information Service (ALIS) found that some subjects were harder than others with standards varying by up to one grade (CEM, 1994). This finding would be supported by many teachers and students in the schools in our study. Dearing asked SCAA and the Curriculum Assessment Authority for Wales to advise him on the implications of the ALIS research.

We turn now to briefly consider the role of AS levels in the sixth form curriculum. We saw in Chapter 1 that AS levels have been the government's preferred means of broadening the academic curriculum. Hopes have been expressed that AS levels would become the 'bedrock of the system' and that a two A level + two AS level package would become if not the norm in the sixth form at least common. AS level entries increased from 35,919 in 1989 to 52,973 in 1992. In 1993 however there was, for the first time since their introduction, a decline in candidate numbers, to 50,315. A generous interpretation would be that AS level candidacies have reached a plateau of around 50,000 entries and this has been confirmed by the 1995 entry figures. Set against the A level entry of 734,623 in 1993 it is evident that AS levels remain a marginal element of the academic curriculum. As with A level a wide range of syllabuses is available and most subjects have some entries. The most popular AS level subjects are General Studies (9,268 candidates), Maths (6,332), Social Sciences (6,145), French (3,175) and English (3,102). We explore the reasons for the slow take-up of AS levels in Chapter 4 and the reasons for choosing to offer particular subjects, but suffice it to say here that a crucial determinant of whether an AS is taken on is its compatibility with an A level syllabus since virtually everywhere AS levels were taught in A level groups.

The vocational curriculum

While the vocational curriculum has been long established in further education colleges it is a relatively recent development in schools, born out of the growth of the 'new sixth' in the late 1970s and early 1980s which itself was largely a response to the collapse of the youth labour market. More systematic provision of vocational education for sixth formers came with the introduction of the Certificate of Pre-Vocational Education in 1984. This one year course, organised jointly by BTEC, City and Guilds and the RSA was introduced into a number of schools as well as colleges and came to cater mainly for 16 year olds for whom A level courses were considered inappropriate and who did not want to opt for more vocationally specific courses. As we shall see in Chapter 5 many of the schools in our study derived useful experience from their CPVE courses when taking on GNVQs. Opinions were divided on the educational merits of CPVE but there was widespread agreement that the course had very little external credibility or visibility. Few employers had heard about it. In the late 1980s CPVE was superseded by City and Guilds DVE and from 1987/88 schools were able to offer BTEC First and National Diplomas. Progression in the provision of vocational courses in many of the schools was through CPVE to DVE to GNVQ, with the introduction of some BTEC courses in some schools. There has been quickening growth in the numbers of sixth formers taking vocational courses. This increased from 1.7 per cent of all 16 year olds in 1988/89 to an estimated 14.3 per cent in 1994/95 (these figures include Foundation, Intermediate and Advanced level GNVQs and their predecessors). In the schools in our survey about one in four students in Year 12 were taking vocational courses. Vocational provision in the schools was in a transitional phase. Some schools, for example that featured in the case study which begins this chapter, had moved rapidly to GNVQ, replacing the DVE and BTEC courses which they had been offering. Other schools were more cautious and had maintained their DVE courses. It was not possible for schools to run both DVE and GNVQ courses but GNVQ and BTEC courses (normally at National level) could coexist. However, it is worth noting that none of the 13 independent schools included in our survey were offering vocational courses nor did they have any immediate plans to do so (although one independent school among our case study schools had a small Advanced GNVQ group). Seven state schools also had no vocational provision in their sixth forms, three of these being selective grammar schools. This virtual absence of vocational courses from independent and selective state schools has clear implications for the

38

achievement of parity of esteem.

The more detailed information on the GNVQ curriculum in the schools will be discussed in Chapter 6. The data revealed a strong bias towards Intermediate courses (77 per cent of enrolments) compared to Advanced level courses (23 per cent). Enrolment by vocational areas is shown by Figure 2.7.

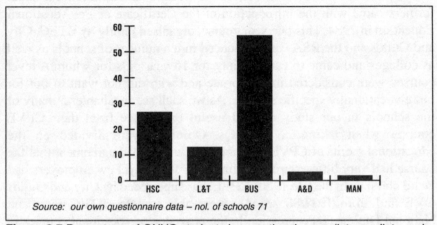

Source: our own questionnaire data – nol. of schools 71

Figure 2.7 Percentage of GNVQ students by vocational areas (intermediate and advanced combined) in North and West Yorkshire schools 1993–1994

Abbreviations: HSC – Health & Social Care; L&T – Leisure and Tourism; BUS – Business; A&D – Art and Design; MAN – Manufacturing

This reflects the patterns of take-up nationally and shows the strong bias, particularly in schools, towards courses in Business and Health and Social Care. Information collected on schools' plans for 1994/95 suggested that this general pattern of provision would continue. Strongest interest was expressed in Business courses (74 courses planned) and Health and Social Care (55 courses) continued to be well represented. Thirty-five courses were planned in Leisure and Tourism. There appeared to be some growth of interest in Art and Design courses and a small number of schools were considering GNVQ Science. Manufacturing, however, continued to be largely ignored and there was also little interest in the areas piloted in 1993/94 and available generally in 1994/95. Most planned courses were at Intermediate level (128 out of 192). There was some evidence of likely growth at Advanced level. We would expect this to continue as students progress through Intermediate level, as much evidence suggests that many of these students are looking to move on to Advanced level. The extent to which this actually happens, however, will be determined both by grading standards at Intermediate level and admission policies for Advanced level.

The core curriculum

In the previous sections we have considered the two types of main courses which students follow in school sixth forms – academic (A and AS levels) or vocational (increasingly GNVQs although with substantial numbers of students continuing to take DVE and BTEC). In addition to these main courses students also participate in a number of other courses and activities which may or may not lead to external certification. It is these activities, separate from the main courses and often compulsory for all sixth formers, upon which we comment briefly in this section. This concept of a core curriculum is connected to, although it does not exhaust, the related idea of 'core skills'. The core skills debate will be rehearsed in some detail in Chapter 7, suffice it to say here that one of the elements in that debate concerns the extent to which core skills, if indeed they can be identified at all, should be taught through main courses or via discrete timetabled curricular units. It is the latter manifestation of the core curriculum with which this section is concerned.

A very wide range of activities were found to constitute the core curriculum. From the questionnaires we recorded almost 30 items which the schools classified as compulsory and almost 50 which were optional. The distinction between the two could not always be easily made. A common pattern was for a school to have some sort of compulsory supplementary or enhancement programme which contained within it optional elements. The sheer variety of activities made it difficult to discern any clear pattern and is itself testimony to the absence of any great consensus among schools as to what should go into the core curriculum.

General Studies, however, remained the mainstay of the core curriculum in many schools, particularly for A level students. The national data for A level entries shown in Figure 2.5 confirm the continued importance of the subject. The fact that General Studies was the most popular AS level subject suggests that some schools are switching from A level to AS level. There was little evidence of much enthusiasm for General Studies among students or teachers. The subject appears to retain its prominence not because anyone particularly wants it but because schools perceive there is nothing better to put in its place.

After General Studies the second most common compulsory element of the curriculum were tutorials. This term can encompass a further wide range of activities and our evidence suggests that there were considerable variations in the seriousness attached to tutorials by students and staff. In some cases tutorial periods were an important element of the sixth form pastoral curriculum, being used perhaps to counsel students, sometimes in conjunction with the recording of achievement. Tutorials were often important for passing on information relating to admission to higher education. Elsewhere, tutorials seem to have amounted to not much more than some desultory hanging about first thing in the mornings before main course lessons began.

Four other common activities will be mentioned briefly, one rather traditional in sixth forms, the other three newer and perhaps evidence of some shifts in the culture of sixth form education. The traditional element was the continued importance of sport and other leisure activities (although the range of activities was often considerably wider than the team games traditionally associated with the sixth form). 'Games' was more likely to be compulsory in independent schools. Of the newer elements one was the growth of work experience, which often took the form of work shadowing. Work experience, of course, is compulsory in many vocational courses, but there was evidence that more A level students were also participating. About 75 per cent of the schools in our survey had work experience in their sixth forms and in about a third of these it was compulsory for some or all of the students. It seems likely that this growth of work experience in the sixth form has come about because of the success of programmes in Years 10 and 11 and the general impetus given to work-related activities by programmes such as TVEI. Information Technology was another common element of the core curriculum. In only a few schools was this compulsory but many offered it as an option, often leading to the RSA's Computer Literacy and Information Technology (CLAIT) certificate. The fourth common activity which featured in about a third of the schools, usually as an option but sometimes as a compulsory element, was community service.

Around a third of schools offered foreign languages as part of their core curriculum, sometimes oriented specifically towards the world of work or business. The languages offered included French, German, Spanish, Italian and Russian.

Apart from the courses and activities listed above there were over 30 others which were offered in the schools. The provision in individual schools often seemed to depend most upon particular interests of members of staff with space on their timetables for some sixth form core work.

In conclusion, our survey of core provision suggests there has perhaps been some shift, with the widespread introduction of work experience, Information Technology and modern languages with a commercial slant, towards a modernised and vocationalised provision. Despite this,

General Studies with its more traditional liberal focus remains the mainstay of much provision. Overall our data suggests the continued paradox of the marginal core. The curriculum, while it contained, nominally at least, some common elements, all too often resembled a rag-bag of provision offering little coherence, which seemed a poor vehicle for carrying the large aspirations of core skills initiatives. In addition, while some heads of sixth forms took core provision seriously and were striving to bring about improvement, our evidence, more fully illustrated in Chapter 6, was that the core curriculum was frequently somewhat despised by students and, allegedly, some staff.

The changing curriculum

Although much of our data inevitably captured a snapshot of the sixth form curriculum, we were also anxious to obtain a sense of the curriculum as a dynamic, changing entity. We asked teachers about the ways in which the curriculum had changed over the previous five years, the plans which the schools had for the following year and asked them to speculate on what the curriculum might be in two or three years' time.

The curriculum was marked by both continuity and change. The academic curriculum was mainly characterised by continuity. When staff reflected on the A level curriculum typical comments were: 'Not much has changed with regard to A levels' and 'It's not much different to what it was ten years ago'. However, it would be incorrect to portray the A level curriculum as being totally resistant to change. There were changes in A levels both at the level of subject titles and in the curricular experiences of students. In terms of subject titles a number of schools had introduced A levels such as Politics, Theatre Studies, Business Studies, English Language, Communications Studies, Performing Arts and Sports Studies. There had also been slow and uneven growth in modular A levels, although there was a good deal of support for the concept of a modular A level course. Taken together these changes perhaps encapsulate a cautious process of modernisation of the A level curriculum involving some diversification and a subtle redefining of the meaning of 'academic'.

We have already noted the relative failure of AS levels to establish themselves as a major component of the academic curriculum. Thus, while there were elements of change within the academic curriculum the overall picture remains substantially one of stability and this well befits the discourse of the 'gold standard' which has surrounded the academic curriculum in recent years. When we asked staff to look ahead two or three years they mainly tended to see the development of the academic curriculum in the schools proceeding along similar incremental lines, with a few new subjects being introduced, a few being dropped and further slow changes in syllabus and assessment arrangements. This was far from being an unwelcome prospect for many teachers and while there was much support for the reform of A level, in a school system beset by change over the last decade, stability and gradual change in the sixth form academic curriculum was welcomed by many.

If the academic curriculum was marked largely by stability the vocational curriculum was characterised by change. This had two main elements: firstly, the vocational curriculum had expanded greatly. Whereas in the early 1980s, where it existed at all in schools, it had consisted of perhaps a dozen CPVE students taught by a small cadre of teachers, by 1992 in many schools it accounted for 25 per cent of sixth formers with a variety of courses on offer involving a substantial proportion of school staff. While the academic curriculum remains the bedrock of the sixth form in most schools, the vocational curriculum is far more significant than it was. Secondly, this expansion has been accompanied by very substantial curriculum development. The progression from CPVE through DVE, sometimes taking in BTEC, to GNVQ, has already been outlined above and will be explored in greater detail in Chapters 5 and 6.

These changes have brought an increasing number of teachers into contact with curricula which call for very different pedagogical and assessment strategies than the GCSE and A level courses with which the teachers were more familiar. Not only this but while there have been elements of continuity within the vocational curriculum there have also been major changes. Thus, while teachers were able to draw upon their experience of CPVE or DVE when taking on GNVQ the new courses were also different in important ways from those which had gone before.

When staff looked ahead two or three years they foresaw the major changes in the sixth form curriculum continuing to be on the vocational side. This would involve the continued conversion from DVE and BTEC to GNVQ and also the continuing expansion of GNVQ through offering more courses and levels.

In addition to asking teachers about the changes which had taken place in the sixth form curriculum we asked why these changes had taken place. The most common response was that new courses had been introduced as a result of student demand. This in itself may be significant, as one of the aims of educational reforms has been to make schools more responsive to their 'market'. Upon closer examination, however, it was clear that there was no simple reaction by schools to student demand. In fact, as often as responding to demand schools were creating it by taking the initiative in introducing and marketing new courses. Certainly a number of the schools had produced glossy, attractive sixth form prospectuses in order to attract students. In addition there was also much informal encouragement by teachers for students to take particular courses. The strengths and experience of staff were also important factors in accounting for changes which took place. The introduction of a new course in the sixth form was a way in which a teacher could make a mark in a school, particularly in view of the high status accorded to sixth forms in general. The appointment of a new member of staff might provide the opportunity to introduce a new course. Similarly the departure of a teacher might result in the disappearance of an established course. Change in the 16–19 curriculum should not be divorced from more general questions related to teachers' careers. Thus the notion of schools responding to student demand concealed complex processes of decision-making in which demand was an important, but not overriding, factor. However, as we have noted above, 16–19 education and training is currently characterised by expansion and buoyancy. Virtually all the schools were thinking in terms of the expansion of their sixth forms. This has important implications for the arguments about the size of sixth forms. There is growing evidence that the rise in staying-on rates in full-time education has peaked or at least is going to increase more slowly. If provision does continue to expand in the ways suggested by our informants this can only heighten competition between institutions and exacerbate the problem of small groups sizes indicated by the Audit Commission report. It remains to be seen how this tension between the current expansion fuelled by the quasi-education market and the imperatives of economy of scale will be worked out in practice.

CHAPTER 3

A Levels on Trial

I could see us actually abandoning A levels eventually in favour of
GNVQ 3 as being more suited to the kind of students we get and more
appropriate to their needs. But there's obviously a kind of cultural thing
as far as the staff are concerned, the A level is a kind of gold standard
in the view of the government, parents and so forth.

(TVEI Co-ordinator in an 11–18 school)

A levels have always been on trial. Introduced in 1951 as single subject
examinations to replace the Higher School Certificate they were accused
from the outset of being overly specialised. Within 15 years proposals for
their replacement were being discussed at a national level (Schools
Council, 1966). Indeed at regular and ever decreasing intervals in the
second half of this century, GCE A level has been declared a problem.
Proposed solutions of interested parties have ranged from abolition to
renovation, though only rarely have proposals gained governmental
acknowledgement let alone approval or action. Thus nearly five decades
after their introduction and in the face of organised and eloquent
opposition GCE Advanced Levels continue to be the reference point of
the 16–19 curriculum.

That the A level examination has even survived, unlike its Ordinary
Level equivalent, indicates the constancy of national policy and
academic practice in respect of the most intellectually able 16–19 year
olds. Whatever the opposition and political manoeuvring beneath the
surface, the public face of government policy in this area has remained
consistent; the value of A levels has been reaffirmed. In recent years, as
criticisms of A levels have proliferated and intensified, further political
capital has been invested in the academic status quo through repeated
ministerial assertion: 'GCE A levels are here to stay' (*DfE News* 376/93),
'The Government remains committed to GCE A levels' (*DfE News*

203/94), 'We remain committed to GCE A levels' (*DfE News* 308/94). While a cabinet minister might feel nervous if such reassurances were given about his or her post, there would appear to be little doubt about the policy position taken by the government's education department in recent years. Indeed the route to respectability for the advanced GNVQ lies, in the Department for Education and Employment's eyes at least, with linkage to the academic reference point of A level. Even in announcing the wide-ranging review of 16–19 education led by Sir Ron Dearing, the Secretary of State stressed the boundaries of the remit: '*nothing* will be allowed to get in the way of protecting the rigour and depth of GCE A levels' (original emphasis) (*DfE News* 79/95). However, the views of the former Department of Employment and of the Department of Trade and Industry on the dominance of A level have traditionally been more ambiguous (*TES*, 3 July 1993).

As will be seen in the following chapter much of the wider debate on A levels, has focused on the need to reformulate GCE A level to broaden the 16–19 curriculum and, more recently, to relocate it in the continuum of compulsory schooling and post-compulsory education and training. The concern of this chapter is, however, to consider the current nature and extent of the 'problems' internal to A levels.

Proposals for A level reform

While successive governments have been loath to accept that there is a problem with A levels they have regularly sought the advice (and reassurance) of their examinations, curriculum and inspection advisory bodies on matters internal to the A level system. In 1988, one notable request for advice on the recommendation of 'principles that should govern GCE A level Syllabuses and their assessment' (DES, 1988, p39) was met with a considered proposal from the Committee chaired by Dr Gordon Higginson for the recasting of the A level system.

Exceeding its brief the Committee put forward an alternative view of A levels, arguing for broader post-16 academic provision in which five 'leaner' yet 'tougher' A levels would form the basis of the standard academic curriculum (DES, 1988, p13). The 'Higginson' Committee sought to develop further the concept of contrasting studies, one of the justifications for the recently introduced AS examinations which were to be examined for the first time in 1989. The proposals in the Committee's report for the five slimmer A levels were immediately rejected by the DES. It was clear that the government's brief had been exceeded and that extensive change post-16 was ill-advised given the recent introduction of the GCSE and the imminent introduction of the National Curriculum together with the other demands on teachers made by the 1988 Education (Reform) Act. The principle of breadth was, however, accepted by the government though it was the new AS level that was seen as the route to widening the academic curriculum.

In September 1988, nearly four months after the publication of *Advancing A Levels*, the new School Examinations and Assessment Council was asked by Secretary of State Kenneth Baker to continue the work undertaken by the previous examinations advisory body 'in the approval of A and AS level syllabuses, in scrutinising these examinations and in working towards a rationalisation of the range of syllabuses on offer' (quoted in SEAC, 1990, p2). The advice of SEAC was also requested on the 'implications' of the 'Higginson Report' though it was again made clear that the way forward was to be sought in the promotion of AS levels. The request led to a major consultation exercise being undertaken by SEAC in the first half of 1989. Over 4,000 questionnaires were sent to institutions and organisations involved in post-compulsory education with a response rate of 22 per cent. The questions in this consultation document focused on breadth in the academic curriculum; the role of AS levels; the nature, content and range of A level syllabuses; the means by which A and AS might be rationalised and developed and the desirability of devising syllabus and examination principles to govern the Advanced level system (SEAC, 1990).

The report on the consultation emphasised the importance attached by respondents to breadth in the post-16 curriculum but also stressed the diverse interpretations of 'breadth' and the difficulties involved in translating these interpretations into practice. This discussion and the views on the role of AS level examinations highlighted in the consultation report will be taken up in the following chapter.

The section in the consultation report on A level examinations described the strong general support for A level particularly in terms of 'intellectual rigour' and the way it was felt to develop 'powers of conceptualisation, abstract and analytical thought and the ability to assimilate knowledge' (SEAC, 1990). The A level was considered to be a benchmark against which to judge current and future academic capability. The report does acknowledge that 'While the strengths of A levels received wide commendation many respondents were at pains to point out that they were referring to the best of advanced level provision' (ibid., p31) and goes on to list and discuss the weaknesses of A level as put forward by respondents. These concerns principally related to the reductionist effect of the knowledge-oriented syllabuses for single subject terminal examinations on teaching and learning. The narrowness of the academic perspective, the excessive factual content and the restricted range of assessment were felt to lack continuity with the students' preceding GCSE courses and to be inappropriate for both further study and employment. A more general criticism was made of the proliferation and variation in subject syllabuses. There was consequently general support for some form of common core and general principles for A level syllabuses. The case was also made for modular syllabuses to link A and AS courses with core modules and to allow for choice and flexibility supported by credit accumulation and transfer.

Development of A and AS level principles

In responding to the Secretary of State's request for advice, SEAC drew upon the consultation responses and recommended the development of general principles for A and AS to rationalise and standardise current syllabus provision and assessment practice, whilst maintaining a policy of encouraging the limited development of alternative syllabuses and forms of assessment such as modular A level schemes. These proposals were subsequently accepted by the next Secretary for State, John MacGregor, who asked SEAC to proceed to the development of A and AS principles (quoted in SEAC, 1990, Document 4).

In September 1990 detailed draft principles were drawn up by SEAC based on the deliberations of four working groups and a widespread consultation focusing on the individual principles was undertaken (SEAC, 1991). The draft principles were revised in the light of the responses though not all contested principles were changed. For example the proposed 40 per cent ceiling for internally assessed coursework was retained despite widespread disagreement with this limitation. The principles were divided into principles relating to syllabuses design (including assessment) and examination procedure before being submitted by SEAC to the Secretary of State in late 1990 who responded in May 1991.

When the *Principles for GCE Advanced and Advanced Supplementary Examinations* were finally published by SEAC in 1992 it became clear that the results of the two extensive and detailed consultation exercises undertaken had been reduced to twelve brief principles. While all explanation of the principles, the guidelines specifying the detail and the procedural principles had been removed, guidance on the implementation of the principles was promised by SEAC. Nonetheless, the pastel shades in the leaflet with reassuring images of students working independently on tasks seemed designed to disguise a shift in the nature and content of the principles. The schools and colleges in supporting SEAC's development of general principles now found that SEAC's proposed internal coursework limit had been reduced from a norm of 40 per cent to a regulatory maximum of 20 per cent of total marks in most subjects. The thrust of the government's thinking on modular courses was revealed by the rewording of the relevant principle from 'Any course made up of modules should be demonstrably coherent' (SEAC, 1991, p116) to 'ensure that any course made up of modules is demonstrably coherent and to the same standard as other A and AS courses' (SEAC, 1992, p3). Other indications of the attitude towards the role of examinations in the maintenance of academic standards could be seen in the replacement of the wording 'A and AS syllabuses should employ a variety of approaches to assessment in order to maximise the range of opportunities for candidates to demonstrate positively what they know, understand and can do' (SEAC, 1991, p117) by the requirement for assessment 'to be predominantly by means of externally assessed terminal examinations' (SEAC, 1992, p4).

A and AS Code of Practice

Upon the recommendation of OFSTED (1993) the following holder of the office of Secretary of State, John Patten, wrote to Sir Ron Dearing at the newly formed SCAA to request a common Code of Practice for Advanced level examinations (*DfE News* 376/93). Thus the guidance and procedures for the conduct of Advanced level examinations promised by SEAC were developed by SCAA in conjunction with the GCE examination boards and published in July 1994 as the *Code of Practice for GCE A and AS Examinations* (SCAA and the GCE Examining Boards of England, Wales and Northern Ireland, 1994). The development of this voluntary Code of Practice built upon the A and AS principles and outlined their implementation.

The Code of Practice includes the requirement of a progressive revision by GCE subject of all Advanced level syllabuses so that they conform to the Code and subject core requirements before approval by SCAA. Internally assessed coursework is confirmed as having a normal limit of 20 per cent of the total marks with eight subjects accepted as exceptions (the highest limit being Art and Design at 60 per cent). With regard to modular examinations it is made clear that each module is to be assessed at the full standard for Advanced level irrespective of whether it is required to be taken early in the course by the stipulated sequence of modules (although the module may be re-sat later in the course). Because of minimum requirements for module weightings (15 per cent of total marks) and for terminal examinations (30 per cent) syllabuses may have no more than six modules of which at least two must be assessed after the examination entry date in the final year. It should be noted though that the definition of terminal examination included the external assessment of modular examinations and practical work.

Meanwhile work had commenced on the development of new subject cores for A and AS Level syllabuses. The need to re-establish the relationship of the A and AS syllabus content and to rationalise an increasing diversity of A level syllabus provision in individual subject areas meant that SEAC undertook a rolling programme to replace the common A level cores (developed in the 1980s) by joint A and AS subject cores. Following the development of these subject cores and the subsequent consultation exercises the first seven syllabuses conforming to the new requirements were introduced in September 1994 with progressive introduction of the remaining sixteen subject cores.

Changes to A levels

In recent years post-16 education and training in general and A level syllabuses in particular have increasingly been the object of strong criticism from a wide range of organisations and educational commentators. As we have seen in Chapter 1 many proposals for reform have been and continue to be put forward. In terms of their varying implications for the future of A level, these proposals fall into different categories.

In the late 1980s the proposals for change in the academic curriculum focused on increasing breadth; the reaffirmation of the centrality of A levels through the introduction of the AS examination; the recasting of A levels recommended by the Higginson Report and the proposed development of core skills. These will be discussed in the following chapter.

In the early 1990s, at a more systemic level, some bodies advocated a single overarching diploma with a minimum qualification requirement to unite separate vocational and academic tracks (e.g. HMC, 1993). This indeed was promulgated as government policy in the White Paper *Education and Training for the 21st Century* jointly produced by the

Department of Education and Science and the Department of Employment in 1991 who put forward the title 'Advanced Diploma' (DES/DOE/Welsh Office, 1991). Under proposals of this type, A level syllabuses would not be altered by the introduction of the additional certification though greater esteem might be conferred on the vocational route together with the possibility of increased breadth through core skills and mixing of qualifications.

Others have proposed a unified version of the present multi-track system with more bridges and ladders between the vocational and academic routes based on a modular structure of credit accumulation and transfer to encourage a less polarised approach (e.g. CBI, 1993). However, as will be seen, significant structural and conceptual changes are needed for A level to take part in a true modular scheme with credit accumulation and transfer.

A third group of proposals has been based on the premise that division is inevitable within a flawed system. Here the unification principle is taken further with calls for the abolition of A level and the replacement of current academic and vocational qualifications by a new qualification system either fully modularised (e.g. Kidd, 1992) or based on a single diploma or baccalaureate with different pathways (e.g. Finegold et al., 1990).

The general agreement on the need for reform indicated in the above proposals leading up to the Dearing 16–19 review was symbolised by a joint statement in October 1994 by six of the leading headteachers and college principals associations (AfC/GSA/HMC/SHA/APVIC/SHMIS, 1994). The joint statement emphasised the view of the associations represented that there should be a 'single national framework' (ibid., p3) with a modular structure. Free-standing modules or units would be 'banked' to accredit achievement and then accumulated towards a longer-term qualification. Importantly, in political terms, the joint statement claimed that the proposed changes 'can evolve from within the present systems' and would 'retain the best of the present structure' (ibid.) highlighting the measures that could be taken to facilitate credit accumulation and transfer. These were given as the lifting of restrictions on A level modular development and assessment so that A level modules could be of different levels and have a weighting system equivalent to vocational qualifications.

The stance adopted in the joint statement was akin to the more pragmatic approach being taken by a number of post-16 curriculum developers. Recognising that the government is publicly committed to the retention of A level reinforced by the rhetorical promotion of the label as a 'beacon of excellence, sending out an unwavering signal to higher education, employers and parents alike' (*DfE News*, 391/93), they have sought to reform A level syllabuses and assessment formats from within. Coursework has been introduced, modular syllabuses have begun to proliferate, new examination formats assessing practical skills have come to the fore and modern syllabuses focusing on areas of learning and experience rather than the traditional academic disciplines have been developed. All these changes have implications for patterns of subject study and approaches to teaching and learning. Perhaps the question should be asked: 'Are A levels what they were or have they changed their nature but not their name?' Indeed is it still appropriate to dismiss them as 'highly specialised and old-fashioned exam-based courses' (Finegold et al., 1990)?

Incremental change?

In order to gauge the extent of actual change at the institutional level, one focus of the research upon which this book is based sought to elicit the views of those with responsibility for sixth form teaching and organisation and of the students on the A level courses. While it is self-evident that the students are not in a position to comment on change over time, they are uniquely qualified to comment on the current experience of A levels and the relationship to the GCSE courses they took. Year 11 students were also interviewed in small groups from their perspective of having to make a choice on their future qualifications path. The teachers interviewed were deputy headteachers or heads of sixth form together with GNVQ or TVEI coordinators. Most of those interviewed had responsibility for teaching GCE A level subjects and were keen to comment on their own subject area as well as on the wider aspects of A levels and curriculum organisation in their sixth form. It is to the principal accusations which have been made of GCE A levels that we will now turn in order to consider these in the light of the views and experiences of those working daily with A levels and to assess the current position.

A high failure rate?

'A levels are a risky investment of time' (Smithers, 1994, p358) is a principal accusation of the unsuitability of A level courses, with high failure rates identified as a major cause for concern by many commentators. Stanton sums up the problem thus: 'Thirty-seven per cent of 16-year-old school leavers get five or more GCSEs at grade A–C, compared with 25 per cent 10 years ago' and 'nearly 35 per cent of the age group take A level compared with 26 per cent a decade ago, but only 22 per cent of the cohort get two passes' (Stanton, 1994, pp244–5). This was a concern addressed by the Audit Commission in a detailed analysis of participation and completion rates in 16–19 education. In 1993 the Commission reported that of those students confirmed as being enrolled on courses on 1 November in a given year 'non-completion rates average about 13 per cent for A level course' with a further 17 per cent unsuccessfully completing the course of at least two A levels (Audit Commission/OFSTED, 1993, p2). While some non-completion may be accounted for by those moving to jobs or different courses, a major concern of the Audit Commission was, understandably, the cost of providing courses on which three students in ten did not achieve the aims of the course, namely to gain at least two A level passes.

Irrespective of the high cost of 'failure' rates, estimated at £500 million for all 16–19 provision, such a significant proportion of A level students failing to gain two A levels serves no good purpose. The problem lies in that neither those who, for whatever reason, leave the course early, nor those who complete but do not gain a pass grade, have any formal recognition of what might be considerable achievement in personal terms. In the case of students who transfer courses or who are compelled to leave the course part-way through because of personal circumstance the achievement may in fact be high in A level's own academic terms.

The most recent figures for A level subject entry (Summer 1995) reveal that 16 per cent of all entries (some 116,000) are not awarded an A–E grade. The figure for science subjects is higher with nearly one in five entries failing. Education Minister Eric Forth, in commenting on the similar results of 1994, turned the figures on their head seeing that a pass rate of 80 per cent was a matter of pride (*TES*, 19 August 1994), the government's position being that the failure rate is indicative of the rigorous academic nature of the examinations. This seems to miss the point expressed succinctly by Sir Christopher Ball that it is a bold nation 'that thinks it can afford to fail at 18 nearly one-third of those identified at 16 as academically most able' (quoted in Kerr, 1992, p45).

In our research the difficulty of A levels as compared to GCSE was felt more acutely by some Year 12 and Year 13 students than others though nearly all thought that the transition from GCSE to A level had been marked by a 'big jump' in difficulty. What differed most, however, was the nature of this difficulty. For some the jump from GCSE to A level had been high because of a necessity to gain a full understanding of concepts rather than to learn and reproduce explanations and facts. Others had experienced problems coming to terms with the wide-ranging scope and greater depth required for subjects. All found the total workload heavy and much increased from pre-16.

The A level science subjects were generally found to be significantly harder than at GCSE, especially by those who had not studied single subject sciences. The widest gap in standards between A level and GCSE was considered to be in Chemistry. Physics and Biology were also felt to be much harder as was Mathematics. Students taking arts subjects were less concerned about the transition from GCSE. For them the level and amount of work was more demanding but did seem to be an extension of GCSE work. Geography was seen to have much more factual content to learn with a greater need for mathematical skills while in History there was much more emphasis on the students finding out information for themselves and on writing essays. English Literature demanded a new style of literary appreciation and essay writing and Modern Languages such as French were found by some students to be particularly difficult though this varied. One school had sought to address what was perceived as a very real gap between GCSE and A level by encouraging departments to adapt the way Year 12 students are taught in the first term and to have an induction course to fill gaps in knowledge and understanding which would have been covered by O level.

There was general agreement amongst sixth form students that while GCSE had felt difficult at the time, looking back it seemed easy and had prepared them inadequately for A levels. They wished they had covered the subject knowledge in greater depth, had been warned of and prepared for the ways of working post-16 particularly with reference to more independent ways of working, the need for self-reliance and motivation and the huge increase in workload. Interestingly, while A levels were universally acknowledged to be demanding in terms of the level and style of work, only a few sixth formers were in favour of bringing A levels into line with GCSE. The consensus was that GCSE syllabuses and teaching needed to extend students more and prepare them for further study and the different methods of working at A level. Several students complained that they had not been given a true picture of A level work and that they had not been psychologically prepared for the huge gap in difficulty. This general feeling was summed up by one Year 12 student:

> I chose subjects that I liked, but nobody told you that A level History will be nothing like GCSE History. Now can't stand History. Big jump from GCSE to A level. It should be explained. No-one explains how

hard it is – they say it's general progression but it's not.

One student commented that even students who get high grades in GCSE might think they can do A levels but that this is giving them a false sense of security.

A level entry requirements

So does the problem of the difficulty of A level for many students lie at the door of inappropriate entry requirements laid down by schools for entry to their sixth form? The Audit Commission in its investigation found that there is a 'marked relationship between prior GCSE results and the non-completion rate' (Audit Commission/OFSTED, 1993, p27) and, unsurprisingly, that 'success at A level correlates well with achievement at GCSE' (ibid., p30). The consequent advice to schools and colleges was that students whose GCSE achievement was beneath four grade Cs and three grade Ds should 'not be admitted to A level courses without being made aware of their low chances of success' (ibid., p27). This suggested minimum entry requirement is in line with that expected by schools in the research project. The general practice was for schools only to admit students to the A level courses if they had at least four GCSEs at grade C though there was some flexibility in individual cases. The range of requirements for GCE A level study varied from three to six GCSEs at grades A–C with some individual departments requiring an A or B grade for a particular subject. However, some schools would permit students with a grade D in a subject to study that subject at A level, sometimes on a trial basis. This flexibility in entry requirements is in fact supported by the figures given by the Audit Commission which indicate that over 40 per cent of students with GCSE grades below the minimum given above do complete the course and, on average, achieve a modest but significant total A level score of some 5 points (where a grade E is weighted at 2 points and a grade D at 4 points).

Confirmation of the inadvisability of relying solely on GCSE scores to predict A level performance comes from the Youth Cohort Study which found that 'summary measures to total GCSE grades did not appear to be such good predictors of A level success as similar summaries of O levels and CSEs had been', suggesting that 'the main reason for this appears to have been that young people with relatively low scores in the post-GCSE cohort did rather better in terms of A level success than similarly poorly-qualified young people in the pre-GCSE cohort' (Ashford et al., 1993, p13). A similar point is taken up by the Government Statistical Service which found that although there was a 'strong link...between a candidate's GCE A/AS level score and the same candidate's score at GCSE' (*DfE Statistical Bulletin* 9/94), it was equally true that 'candidates with similar levels of performance at GCSE achieved a wide range of GCE A/AS level scores (ibid., para. 2).

The DfE has sought to assist initial grade prediction (as well as curriculum planning and resource targeting) at the local and national level by publishing *GCSE to GCE A/AS Value Added: Briefing for Schools and Colleges* (DfE, 1995). This document, accompanied by a technical briefing, provides national data in the form of graphs of matched GCSE/GCE results to enable curriculum managers to compare their students' performance against the national picture in terms of value added between the two examinations.

The implications of the points discussed above for careful and appropriate student guidance are discussed further in Chapter 8 though it is worth pointing out at this stage that the Audit Commission report also highlights the findings of studies by HMI that 'even where most students were well qualified to tackle A level, many were doing so in subjects where their previous attainments had been modest, and over 50 per cent chose at least one new subject for which they had no qualification' (Audit Commission/OFSTED, 1993, p27). One example of an A level subject not commonly offered pre-16 is Economics. Predictably students taking this subject for the first time commented on difficulty though this did not seem to be a problem for those that had taken GCSE Economics.

Thus, while the application of a minimum entry qualification might appeal in an attempt to raise successful completion rates, caution must be applied not to make the entry requirements too inflexible nor too strict given the uncertainty of using GCSE results as sole predictors of A level performance. Perhaps surprisingly the publication of a school's A level results in terms of the proportion of A level students passing two A levels did not arise as a major issue in our research though the pass rate was one of the considerations in the setting of minimum entry requirements. Schools are clearly keen to ensure that students do not embark upon a course at which they are likely to fail though the uncertainty highlighted above coupled with pressure from students influenced by the status of A levels can be difficult to resist.

Narrow academic syllabus content

The academic curriculum as a whole has been criticised for over specialisation and narrowness as will be seen in Chapter 4. However, the same accusations have also been levelled at the content of individual A level courses. Syllabuses have been said to neglect important skills and to be irrelevant to the needs of society, even of Higher Education – their *raison d'être*. As seen above such criticisms were identified by the SEAC consultation in 1989 where the principal internal weaknesses of A levels were put forward as being their 'narrow academic orientation with an unwarrantedly restrained knowledge base' and their 'over-burdened content, sometimes unrelated to the real world' (SEAC, 1990, p32). However, recent years have seen a rapid increase in candidate numbers in new subject areas many of which are interdisciplinary in nature and do not fit neatly into the traditional academic categories.

While A level subject entries increased overall by some 19 per cent between Summer 1989 and Summer 1993 as the post-16 staying-on rate rose, the corresponding rise for some non-traditional subjects was much higher. The most significant increases during this period in terms of candidate numbers were in Sociology (21,730 to 31,577), Business Studies (6,977 to 22,678) and Psychology (6,440 to 16,322) with a host of smaller subject entries experiencing high percentage increases including Sports Studies, Politics and Political Studies, Media Studies, Theatre Studies and Communication Studies. Psychology and Business Studies have registered further significant increases between 1993 and 1995 as have Sports Studies and Media Studies. However, as the FEFC points out, there are wide variations in levels of subject entry between types of institution. For example, the area of Social Studies 'is the most popular subject in general further education and tertiary colleges with 23 per cent of all entries, but (in 1994) it accounts for only ten per cent of sixth form college entries and five per cent of school entries' (FEFC, 1994b, p9).

Despite the caution expressed above, there was considerable interest in the schools in our research in the non-traditional subjects and newer subjects such as English Language (7,860 entries in 1993) though few as yet had made significant changes to their GCE A level subject provision other than adding two or three of these subjects to the existing curriculum. Some heads of sixth form stressed that the new less-traditional subjects had been introduced in response to student demand. One commented:

A lot of the students that were doing Economics were saying 'Well I'd quite like to have been able to do Politics or Sociology to go with the Economics' and so with quite a number of students indicating that that was something that they would like to have done we listened to that and then tried to put those A level courses on for those students. They've got a group of about 18 students. So the new courses seem to have bedded in quite nicely and be towards the top end of the numbers that are taking subjects. I'd say definitely pupil demand and parental demand for new courses has then allowed us to look at whether or not we could provide those courses and we've managed to be able to do that. That hasn't been at the expense of any other course which has gone in the sixth form.

Schools clearly feel a need to offer as wide a range of GCE A level subjects as possible to retain students in their sixth form who are looking to take A level courses in non-traditional subjects. Indeed several Year 11 students commented that they would be leaving against their general wish in order to study subjects at college that weren't on offer in their school. This was most frequently the case with A level Psychology and, to a lesser extent, Sociology.

The trend towards expansion of the newer A level subjects such as Media Studies, Sports Studies and Business Studies has meant that these multidisciplinary syllabuses with their emphasis on greater integration and application of knowledge allied to elements of project and practical work are now forming part of the A level curriculum for a higher proportion of the increasing numbers of students. In the same period of 1989 to 1993 these increases in entry numbers for non-traditional subjects are being matched in the growth in numbers taking the revised or new syllabuses in the more traditional subjects of A level (e.g. 16–19 Geography from 2,100 to 11,869). Indeed, as we have seen in Chapter 2, it is often the new subjects and the new syllabuses which show the most dramatic increases in numbers of candidates whereas entry rates for some of the traditional subject syllabuses have remained static or only increased slightly despite the significant increase in A level entries.

Assessment formats

A level syllabuses have frequently been criticised for their narrow assessment methods, namely terminal written examinations with a focus on knowledge and factual recall. However, the growth and popularity of the new subjects and syllabuses identified above is partly attributable to changes in assessment formats that have taken place in recent years. These developments can be said to fall into two main, but interlinked, categories: coursework and modular syllabuses.

Coursework

As the internally assessed coursework element pre-16 increased with the introduction and development of GCSE syllabuses, the pressure from schools and colleges on the examination boards to limit the dependence on terminal examinations post-16 bore some fruit. Arising out of the work undertaken by syllabus developers such as the Schools Council subject groups an increasing number of syllabuses have been developed with a project or coursework element. In 1993 HMI were able to report that, of 60 syllabuses analysed as part of their DfE instigated inspection, a coursework element is available (though usually not compulsory) in the majority of syllabuses.

Coursework or project elements in syllabuses have found favour with many teachers, lecturers and students for their emphasis on the assessment of carefully planned, prepared and presented project or topic work that is relevant to the students' own context, experience and interests. This practical focus and relevance, together with the more immediate assessment format and decreased reliance on terminal examinations, has had a beneficial effect on motivation. An internal briefing note from SCAA's post-16 team sums up the position:

> In some subjects, it is important for candidates to be able to show what they know, understand and can do in a way that is not possible in the closely controlled conditions of an examination room. This might involve a variety of activities including, for example, fieldwork, research, experimental and oral work. Coursework can be particularly motivating and allow candidates to display skills of diligence and perseverance.

(SCAA post-16 team, *A/AS Coursework* Briefing Note, December 1993)

This view is confirmed by FEFC who in their 1994 national survey on A and AS levels reported that 'many students are articulate, hard-working and committed. This was particularly evident in extended coursework or project work' (FEFC, 1994b, p18).

HMI found in their analysis of syllabuses in 1993 that the proportion of the coursework element in syllabuses 'can vary from 10 per cent to, exceptionally, 75 per cent, but it is commonly about 20 per cent' (OFSTED, 1993, p16). In limiting the normal coursework proportion of a syllabus to 20 per cent the GCE examinations boards' voluntary Code of Practice conforms to the government's principles for A and AS level examinations and would seem to be in line with the norm to be found in A level syllabuses. However, a closer examination reveals that the Code of Practice's exceptions to the normal limit of 20 per cent are to be found only in some of the more practical A level subjects such as Art and Design (60 per cent), Design and Technology (50 per cent), Music (50 per cent), Home Economics (40 per cent) and Physical Education (30 per cent) as well as subjects in the general areas of media, communication and the expressive and performing arts (40 per cent). New syllabuses developed in the more traditional subjects as well as those in applied and vocational areas must conform to the 20 per cent coursework limit with substantial revisions necessary to many existing syllabuses and consequent implications for teaching and learning methods and student motivation.

The almost arbitrary limitation on coursework at A level (and at GCSE) arises from the government's barely concealed lack of confidence in the reliability of teacher assessment as personally expressed by the Prime Minister, John Major. The suspicion expressed is that coursework is easier than an examination and that it is in danger of undermining the rigorous standard of the A level qualification. The government's public commitment is to the maintenance of the A level standard and rather than to the improvement of achievement. As Spours points out: 'higher performance due to coursework tends to reduce the exclusive nature of an academic award and it is precisely this form of selection which has been historically dominant in English qualifications' (Spours, 1993, p151).

Several sixth form teachers in our survey expressed disappointment with the government's attitude to coursework. One commented:

We feel really that A levels with a coursework component are under threat and in the end we wonder whether we're going to be forced back into a situation where the bulk of A levels is going to be examined at the end of two years.

There was general agreement among teachers that coursework was not eroding standards and was certainly not an easy option, benefiting good or very good students at least as much, if not more, than those on the pass–fail borderline:

It's easy to go along the line of thinking that students do better when producing their own coursework. I think actually for the average student it's quite difficult; very able students can produce marvellous research assignments and coursework, but it's quite difficult for average and below average A level students to do that. I think the solid, classic syllabus that we do at English A level is much more structured and suits those students.

Students also thought that coursework could be more challenging than a terminal examination, especially with the emphasis in some subjects on preparing and writing extended essays as part of their coursework. As one teacher commented: 'they're not very good at getting themselves organised'.

Modular A levels

Perhaps the single most important change internal to the A level system has been the development of modular syllabuses, not simply in terms of their structure but because, having in many cases been developed from first principles, they incorporate new ways of teaching and learning often influenced by GCSE. The rapid expansion of these schemes both in terms of the range and number of syllabuses available and the huge increases in student numbers testifies to their popularity and this was confirmed by the schools in our research project. Teachers felt the new modular syllabuses offered students greater flexibility and made the transition from GCSE less traumatic.

The early modular A level schemes were often developed by regional consortia in conjunction with GCE boards and included the twelve 'Wessex' A level syllabuses which had 40 per cent internal assessment (see Rainbow, 1993). While many of the modular schemes have survived the restrictions on coursework introduced by the A and AS principles and consolidated in the Code of Practice, these particular developmental A levels have been discontinued by the Associated Examining Board. The decision to cease this pilot project was taken to the disappointment of schools and developers amid suggestions that the uncertainty of approval by SEAC reflected the government's equivocal attitude to modular schemes in general and to this trail-blazer in particular (*TES*, 30 April 1993).

Though the Code of Practice may have restricted the scope of innovative schemes and of the coursework element in A levels, it has not ultimately curtailed the expansion of the provision and uptake of modular syllabuses. In fact in incorporating the rationalisation of the A and AS subject cores and in laying down the ground rules for the minimum size of modules and the maximum amount of coursework the Code of Practice may ironically have given a boost to modular development. Modular syllabuses now have a greater uniformity of structure by having to conform to the 20 per cent limit on internal assessment (with increased examining board moderation), the 15 per cent minimum size for modules and the 30 per cent minimum requirement for terminal examination. In practice this has meant the maximum and typical number of modules is now six with two being externally assessed after the examination entry date in mid-February. The assessment of the modules is, however, principally by unseen examinations taking place at two or three points each year though this may include externally set and examined practical or oral tests.

Several of the original modular A level syllabuses have been restructured and have been joined by many other syllabuses with a modular format developed since the Code of Practice and introduced in September 1994 with SCAA approval. In some cases more traditional syllabuses have been reformulated with the previous papers and options presenting a new modular structure. This reformulation has brought with it the advantages of shorter-term goals, earlier indication of success and the 'banking' of credits as the course progresses. There is also greater choice though in many cases this is at the institutional level rather than for individual students. One significant constraint, apart from the limit on coursework assessment, has been the fact that the modules, at whatever point they are taken in the course, are examined at the full Advanced level. This contrasts with the stepped levels in many higher education modular schemes, though there is the possibility of non-terminal A level modules being re-taken to improve grades. It is also fair to say that there is already concern at the expense of setting, administering and marking modules at up to three points in the year without the added complexity of stepped levels which would not only increase examination costs but decrease the flexibility of teaching arrangements.

Some examination boards have developed modular provision further by offering new integrated schemes of related modules which may be taken in prescribed combinations and sequences to lead to the accreditation of AS level, A level or multiple A level awards. One example of such a scheme is the GCE Advanced science provision of the Northern Examinations and Assessment Board (NEAB) which covers Science, the specialist sciences and related sciences including Psychology. These subject area modular schemes offer greater flexibility of routes and accreditation than a closed subject scheme as credits accumulated can count towards different GCE subject qualifications. This can be particularly important for students who choose to change direction or the weighting of their subjects. As Moon points out, 'The assessment process can be diagnostic allowing targets to be reformulated whilst safeguarding the value of credits already completed' (Moon, 1988, p8). Some schools in our research project planned this flexibility into individual programmes with decisions on the A or AS only being made at the end of Year 12. Such schemes also have obvious benefits for schools and colleges that wish to co-teach to maximise teaching resources and to keep individual students' choices open as long as possible.

Despite the introduction of the restrictions in the Code of Practice, continuing governmental concern that modular syllabuses entail lower standards led to the commissioning by SCAA of a report from the Curriculum Evaluation and Management Centre (CEM) at Newcastle

University on the comparability of A level performance. This report suggested that results and pass rates in modular A levels were significantly higher than for standard A level courses (*TES*, 20 January 1995). However, caution must be applied to this finding as previous research from Newcastle indicated 'If some syllabuses consistently resulted in greater motivation and higher performance this could not be distinguished, statistically, from lenient grading' (CEM, 1994, p8). Further research into standards and consistency of assessment in modular A levels has been proposed by the 16–19 review.

Teaching and learning styles

The relatively short two year A level courses are often regarded as being dominated by the narrow assessment methods of the terminal examinations with their focus on a high level of subject content. With the advent of the newer subjects and syllabuses and the increase in modular structures and more widespread incidence of coursework, one focus of the research was to investigate teacher perception of change in the students' experience of A level courses.

Heads of sixth form tended to admit that their comments on teaching and learning in their school were influenced to some extent by their own subject teaching and indeed the opinions expressed varied widely as can be seen in the following two comments in similar schools:

> In the main, I would think that the way of learning and the whole process is pretty much the same as it was 20-odd years ago, very much so.

> People think A levels same as they were 10 or 15 years ago but few are, most have adapted to some degree, some are unrecognisable, different ways of doing things.

The general view, however, was that some of the newer A level subjects and the new modular syllabuses have begun to change the nature of the teaching and learning, quite significantly in some cases, and that even in the more traditional syllabuses some degree of change was taking place through the influence of other pre- and post-16 courses:

> I think it has changed, we have learned more...probably from vocational courses. We feel that the experience that the students on vocational courses have are experiences which all students should have, so that's probably having a spin-off in the teaching and learning styles that people have adopted.

This view is balanced by the findings of FEFC who reported that 'Students taking a GCE A level subject in combination with vocational courses often find difficulty in adjusting to the styles of teaching and assessment at GCE A level which are narrower in scope' (FEFC, 1994b, p6).

The key to understanding any changes in teaching styles may well lie with the attitude and approach of the individual teacher or department more than with the subject or syllabus. This is the finding of the statistical analysis of students' views on A level courses undertaken by CEM who found that 'A level teaching styles vary quite dramatically from subject to subject, and also from classroom to classroom, but these differences are not systematically related to syllabuses within a subject' (CEM, 1994, p15). In this respect one head of sixth form in our research commented:

> It depends on how courses are taught as much as which particular course is chosen. I don't think the crusty, traditional caricature is particularly accurate. You can use a straight A level paper but still teach in a very varied and interesting way. I think it has changed, the style of teaching, in the last ten years.

Although it is clearly the case that teachers who feel that traditional courses do not offer what they want 'opt for more varied and innovative styles of examination (including modular schemes) which they consider will appeal to a broader student entry and which they judge will provide good continuity with students' earlier learning' (OFSTED, 1993, p39), it is also true that many schools in our research had not yet made wholesale changes in terms of adopting modular syllabuses though some were intending to make changes in several subject areas.

The view of the A level students of their current courses was surprisingly consistent from school to school. With one or two exceptions, they very clearly felt that at GCSE the emphasis was on factual recall rather than understanding. At A level they were struggling to come to terms with the emphasis that was placed on them to find out information for themselves and to understand underlying concepts. Subject teachers agreed that there was a desire for reliance on the teacher at A level and commented that it seemed to come about in those students who had only just passed GCSE and who were used to being spoon-fed.

While many students found adapting to the new ways of working hard, criticisms of A level teaching styles were few and far between. Only in one school was there obvious dissatisfaction with the A level courses. Perhaps significantly this was a school in which the head of sixth form commented that although there were innovative courses available, the sixth form staff in this comprehensive school were comfortable with fact-based, traditional teaching methods. This attitude in some schools is confirmed by HMI who found that 'A few departments acknowledged that they play safe and continue with long established syllabuses, either because they are satisfied with the result achieved or because staff are comfortable with the styles of teaching and learning required' (OFSTED, 1993, p39).

Many other staff in schools had embraced the new modular A levels with relief and one school had sought to go further and develop a more radical sixth form provision to try and 'change A level experience and move students away from the idea that it's the last bit that counts and actually help students take control of their learning a lot earlier'. Drawing on the experience of offering BTEC courses the school had introduced its own programme of modularisation of A levels, not specifically in terms of offering modular syllabuses, but through the identification of component parts. At the end of each component the work was assessed with achievement recorded to allow monitored progression and to build in a formal opportunity to devise subject-based action plans. The programme, which aims to change teaching and learning styles at A level, was being introduced throughout the academic sixth form after successful piloting in two subjects – one with a modular syllabus, the other with a traditional syllabus.

The present eclectic approach to the opportunities presented by the wide variety of syllabuses available within the main subjects was summed up succinctly by one head of sixth form:

> Institutionally A levels have not forced changes in terms of, say, teaching and learning styles, coursework, internal assessment of practical skills, etc. The framework has changed such that it's inevitable that there will be major change. The notion that A levels have changed radically is probably not viable.

Looking forward

The accusation frequently levelled against A level syllabuses of the narrowness of traditional subject content, assessment formats and teaching methods continues to hold to some extent, though it is equally clear that the experience of A levels is shifting beneath the surface of the sacrosanct label. In the eyes of teachers A level is changing its nature incrementally not only as teaching and learning styles are evolving more generally under the influence of GCSE and vocational courses, but as syllabuses are revised and alternative syllabuses and new subjects are introduced. Schools and colleges are responding to student demand accelerating this change by the adoption of new syllabuses and subjects which are in turn showing a disproportionately high increase in student numbers.

While the changes in the academic curriculum are not radical, as the quotation at the end of the last section suggested, and are certainly not sweeping enough for some heads of sixth form interviewed, the overall result is that the incidence of practical work, coursework, modular assessment, applied and vocational subjects is demonstrably much higher than it was at the beginning of the 1990s. Furthermore even before the Dearing 16–19 review a new structure was beginning to emerge with a developing A level modular framework (though it was as yet incoherent with modules of idiosyncratic weighting and length and all at one level). The Northern Examinations and Assessment Board's (NEAB) modular science scheme for A and AS levels demonstrates how whole areas of the academic curriculum are capable of being modularised to link with a system of credit transfer to other subject areas, other examination boards and more importantly the vocational modular framework linking GNVQs and NVQs.

This creeping modernisation of A levels, however limited, has not escaped the attention of successive government education departments who have made a number of attempts to restrict A level curricular development. This protective attitude even permeated the long overdue 16–19 review which, though welcome in its wide-ranging investigation into the possibilities for increased post-16 coherence, fell short of taking a fresh look at the purposes and syllabus content of A levels, indeed of the justification for the A level system as a whole. Accepting the remit to retain A levels and maintain their 'rigour', Dearing's work in respect of GCE A levels focused on standards and forms of assessment giving particular emphasis to the comparability of standards between subjects, over time and between modular and terminal assessment. Little has been said about the suitability or otherwise of the current academic curriculum to prepare young people for a rapidly changing world of higher education and employment.

Though the case against A levels has not been brought by the government, the public trial may yet take place. Ironically, it was Further and Higher Education Minister, Tim Boswell, who reminded delegates at the 'Future of A levels' conference that the value of qualifications

...is established by the 'market place', and needs to be earned. And value will depend to a large extent on a clear understanding amongst the 'users' – particularly higher education and employers – of what the qualification means – means in terms of knowledge, skills and understanding, and the kind of experience that the holder will have had.

(Boswell, 1994)

66

What may have slipped his mind is that schools, colleges and students are also users and will equally 'shop at the qualifications 'market" (*DfE News*, 107/94). To limit the development of a more modern and relevant A level system in the face of market forces may ultimately be to hasten its demise.

CHAPTER 4

Broadening the Academic Curriculum

There was almost unanimous agreement by the heads of sixth form interviewed in the 20 schools in the research project that the academic curriculum taken by their students was too narrow:

> What we're turning out is quite narrow students in some respects. Obviously there are other students who will maintain an interest in the arts or the sciences, but I don't think it's healthy really to ask them to specialise in so few subjects at this stage.

This supports the findings of the Higginson Committee which reported that the most frequent criticism of A levels presented to them was that the programmes of study were too narrow and that the system encouraged premature specialisation (DES, 1988).

As we saw in the previous chapter the A level syllabuses taken by many students have been introduced or revised since the 1980s though the problem of lack of breadth across subjects remains nearly as acute despite the growth in the numbers of students taking mixed A levels rather than three sciences or three arts subjects.

A small number of those responsible for the sixth form curriculum did, however, reject the notion that breadth lay solely in the variety and number of subjects studied and argued for a more skills-based curriculum. One commented that 'whether it's a three A level or five A level course is not so relevant to students here, it's way the courses are taught and what is expected that's the problem' and another argued:

> A level doesn't meet students' needs, doesn't address all sorts of things like numeracy, communication skills, reasoned hypotheses. These sorts of things are missing within A levels. I'd prefer to go with core skills and meeting individual needs rather than saying 'must broaden curriculum'.

For others the role of A level General Studies or a minority studies programme was important in broadening the structure of the 16–19 academic curriculum. These issues in the debate on core curriculum provision and recent developments in core skills will form the subject of a later chapter. However, for many the problem of lack of breadth does indeed lie with a restricted range of subjects taken by individual A level students leading to over-specialisation and a narrow understanding of the world. The solution is seen in increasing both the number and range of subjects taken. We will thus concentrate here on the views of teachers and students on the relative merits of compulsory or optional breadth as represented by the baccalaureate model which entails the disregard or abolition of A levels and the imposition of breadth with a degree of choice and by the Higginson proposals which were centred on the reform of A levels and the principle of flexibility with breadth being optional. We will then turn to Advanced Supplementary levels, in order to explore the reasons for their limited success and consider their future role.

Students' views on curriculum breadth

It is worth noting at this stage that several heads of sixth form predicted that any move to broaden the curriculum would be unpopular with their current A level students. This was confirmed in interviews with the students in each school. There was widespread resistance to the compulsory broadening of the sixth form academic curriculum and the strong consensus was in favour of the status quo, with only isolated dissenting voices. Several students felt that since they were in the sixth form of their own free choice they should be able to decide which subjects they studied and which not: 'You've come here to do what you want to do, not what someone else wants you to do'. This view was echoed by a Year 11 student: 'The whole thing at A level is to choose what you want to do'.

In their choice of which A levels to take students had been influenced by their GCSE grades, interest in the subject and in some cases their future plans. A significant positive influence for several students had been the teacher who would be taking the course even if this was in a new or different subject. Generally speaking parents had not sought to bring a strong influence to bear though there were isolated cases of pressure to avoid non-traditional subjects or to take sciences.

Students tended to feel little pressure from the school or careers service to do particular subject combinations and some said they had been encouraged by the school to choose the subjects they are good at and enjoy as well as keep their options open. Some students reported deliberately choosing contrasting subjects to keep a broader perspective. A clear trend towards mixed A levels was noted by heads of sixth form; as one put it, 'strange combinations are appearing more frequently'.

For the current A level students the overwhelming view was that the three subjects they were studying were demanding enough intellectually and also in terms of time and organisation. Furthermore they felt that it was important to study the subjects in depth and to maintain standards. In fact it was the very difficulty of specialised study and therefore, they felt, the value of A levels which seemed to appeal to them. This is perhaps not as surprising as it might seem at first if we consider that they are the sixth formers who are most likely to benefit from the current system, if they succeed.

Compulsory breadth?

From the introduction of the A level examination, some academics pointed out that the specialisation of the post-16 curriculum did not follow the pattern of most other western countries – which tended to offer a much broader-based curriculum – until a later stage.

In the revised French *Baccalauréat* system (examined for the first time in 1995) the choice of the different baccalaureate pathways has been restricted to seven – three general education and four technical education pathways. Students on the former route entering *Première* (Year 12) choose between three broad pathways ('Science', 'Economic and Social Studies' or 'Liberal Arts and Language'), the choice of pathway being largely determined by the student's options in the previous year. In each pathway students follow either six or seven compulsory subjects plus at least one subject chosen from a list of specialist options. Thus all students on this academic route must study at least seven or eight subjects (and sometimes choose to take more). Subject breadth is represented not only in terms of the number of subjects taken but by the fact that within each of the three pathways the following subjects are compulsory: French, a modern language, history/geography, physical education. It is interesting to note that mathematics as such does not form part of the compulsory curriculum for the 'Liberal Arts and Language' students at 17+ though they do have to study general science. In the following year *Terminale* students follow a similar pattern with seven compulsory subjects plus in-depth study of a specialist area within their general pathway.

One baccalaureate option available to schools and colleges in the UK is that of the International Baccalaureate, though it is offered by very few centres. Six subjects, each from a different area of the curriculum, must be studied. All students take a first and a second language, a mathematical subject, a science, a humanities subject, economics or social studies plus an option. Three or four of these subjects are studied as higher level courses and the remainder as subsidiary courses with further minority course requirements. As with the French *Baccalauréat* the students may elect to follow a general pathway through their choice of higher level subjects and use the subject option to give it a specialist focus. Thus within the compulsory breadth of a wide range of subjects a degree of specialisation is possible.

How then would teachers and students view the baccalaureate version of a broad academic curriculum? Eight of the twenty heads of sixth form interviewed during our school visits spontaneously mentioned general approval of the baccalaureate, in terms of compulsory broadening of the curriculum. One saw it as the means to a more radical unification of academic and vocational courses based around GNVQ modules and modular A levels. Despite the general agreement that it could be worth exploring the opportunities for wider and more balanced subject coverage encompassed in a baccalaureate qualification, one head of sixth form suspected there might be as many views as there are A level teachers and another highlighted the different perspectives of subject teachers and curriculum managers:

> As a subject specialist I'm reluctant, because I know that means I'll have more people doing some Maths and would not teach to the same level as at the moment, from that perspective I quite like the present system but as Head of Sixth Form it's got to be broader.

Another head of sixth form who would welcome a compulsory broader subject base did also express caution that to have every A level student doing Mathematics, English and a Modern Language would require a change in staffing and be more expensive. A colleague in another school was in favour of the International Baccalaureate but felt that if there was a broader A level course it would have implications for teaching of subjects lower down the school as many pupils came to the sixth form uninspired, even bored, by many of their GCSE subjects. The sixth formers' natural desire to concentrate on the subjects in which they found enjoyment and success was apparent in the interviews: 'You choose A levels that you want so you'll enjoy them whereas for GCSE you had to do them whether you liked them or not'.

Some commented that if they were forced to take a subject they wouldn't be motivated by it. Mathematics and English were mentioned several times in this context. These students felt that although they might have more subjects, they would still end up concentrating on some anyway. A number of students would clearly have experienced some difficulty in identifying more than three subjects they wished to pursue. A minority of others, particularly those who had found difficulty in narrowing their A level choice down to three subjects, had mixed views on a broader A level course as they would have to make a less drastic choice. Nevertheless they did suspect that they would be less well-prepared for university. This lack of preparation for specialised higher education courses was also a concern of some heads of sixth form though it was felt that there was a need for the reconsideration of the purpose of 16–19 education given that a significant proportion of A level students do not proceed to higher education.

Optional breadth?

The Higginson Report specifically rejects the imposed breadth and relative inflexibility of a baccalaureate-type system. In proposing a reduction in the content of A level syllabuses so that five single subject A levels became the norm, the Committee did not even go as far as suggesting that five A levels be compulsory, nor indeed that they must be in contrasting areas: 'students should be free to choose the number of subjects they take and to select the subjects which correspond with their interests, abilities and perceived needs' (DES, 1988, para. 3.13).

While recognising (and approving) the fact that some students would wish to specialise by studying all their subjects in the same general area, it was, nonetheless, a clear hope of the Higginson Committee that students would not restrict their choice of five A levels to just one area and that they would benefit from 'better choice, better opportunities for balance and greater breadth' (ibid., para. 3.5). So would teachers and students be in favour of the 'opportunities and encouragement' (ibid., para. 3.14) to broaden the academic curriculum provided by a greater number of 'leaner' A levels?

By and large the Higginson proposals had found favour with the heads of sixth form though there were some concerns about the reduction in content being seen as unsatisfactory by Higher Education institutions. One head of sixth form admitted to being 'bitterly disappointed when Higginson was rejected' and there was a general agreement that if radical restructuring of the sixth form curriculum to a modular structure or to a baccalaureate system was politically unacceptable then a model based on a wider base of A and AS subjects would be a reasonable compromise. Though here again the subject discipline allegiance of A level teachers was emphasised together with the danger of trivialising experience through the study of too many 'slimmer' subjects.

As with the adoption of a baccalaureate, the resistance of students to even the expectation of an increase in the number of subjects was strong. Many students welcomed the opportunity to concentrate on three subjects. However, the flexibility in the range and number of subjects involved in Higginson's proposals was welcomed both by those who wished to specialise and drop all other subjects as well as by those who had not appreciated having to reduce their subjects from nine or ten to just three especially where they had felt constrained to study in just one area of the curriculum for entry to a particular type of degree course. One sixth former commented: 'Good to have the choice whether to specialise or not, if you know what to do could specialise, if not keep broader course'. This final comment highlights the dilemma inherent in the Higginson proposals that a flexible system holds no guarantee of subject breadth or balance. The same is also true of the Advanced Supplementary levels.

Breadth through AS levels?

'Where schools and students wish to make use of them, Advanced Supplementary (AS) examinations offer a mechanism by which A level work can be broadened while retaining the same mode of study and common standards' (DfE, 1994, p309). This reassuring statement by the former Department for Education echoes the government's repeated rejection of criticism of the lack of breadth in the academic curriculum by reminding detractors of the intended role of AS level syllabuses which were examined for the first time in 1989:

> AS levels are designed to broaden A level students' studies by providing the opportunity for them to continue more of the subjects that they have studied up to the age 16 – or to take new ones. The choice of *contrasting* AS levels – say, English for science students or mathematics for humanities students – will be of particular value in broadening studies. *Complementary* AS levels – say, design and technology for science students – will also offer opportunities for broadening an area of study. (Original emphasis)
>
> (DES, 1986, p1).

The intention was that students would increasingly study four subjects, either with an additional AS level subject or by replacing one of their A level subjects by two AS levels thus broadening their field of study.

However the anticipated attraction of these formulae has not been reflected in the numbers of subject entries. In Summer 1995, six years after the first AS examination took place, the subject entry remains stable at around 50,000 subject entries compared to over 700,000 entries for A level subjects.

The government's reassurance above that AS levels offer a route to breadth, therefore, has begun to look misplaced in the light of the low take-up of AS levels and the realisation that in very many cases neither schools nor students 'wish to make use of them'. Furthermore it is questionable whether those students that have been offered and chosen to follow AS syllabuses are doing so in order to increase subject breadth across the curriculum.

Reflecting the national picture AS level examinations have met with varying degrees of success in the sixth forms in our research project. Indeed several schools had either taken a clear-cut decision not to offer AS levels or did make AS available but did not market it actively to students. It is fair to say that even where a school had made a commitment to offer and promote a wide range of AS levels the enthusiasm of students was muted and the take-up limited. In these schools staff had been disappointed by the students' lack of interest. Some schools considered that their students saw no particular reason to move away from the three A levels and take an additional subject at AS level, seeing it very much as an optional extra which involved a significant amount of work for little tangible gain. Likewise the 2A plus 2AS level model was felt by students to involve too heavy a workload. As one sixth former put it: 'We're encouraged to do it (AS), but only a few do, the majority do three A levels. Better to do three A levels. If you're going to do two years, might as well do A level'.

Thus the general pattern in schools was one of a limited range of AS levels taught to small numbers of students. The actual subjects offered tended to vary according to the particular interests and enthusiasm of individual subject departments. So what then was the role of AS levels in the broadening of the schools' academic curriculum?

HMI in its first evaluation of AS levels argued for a clarification of breadth in the curriculum and the role of AS:

> There are a number of issues to resolve, not least of which is what is meant by a broad curriculum. The evidence points to the fact that there is as yet no consensus on how breadth of study might be achieved and the specific role of AS-examinations within 16–19 students' programmes.

(HMI, 1989, pp7–8)

and reiterated their concern in the review of 1990–91 stating that 'there is need for greater understanding and recognition of their purpose and standard if further progress is to be made' (HMI, 1992, p9) and that 'students are using AS flexibly but not necessarily to broaden significantly their programme of advanced study' (HMI, 1992, p5).

Thus a lack of clarity of purpose, or perhaps an attempt to fulfil a broadening role not appreciated by students, seemed to be leading to a 'misuse' of the possibilities of AS level. One of HMI's principal findings was that where AS levels were taken this was not generally in contrast to a student's A level subjects. In fact in three-quarters of cases the AS level was in a subject area complementary to the student's other subjects. This was most frequently the case with AS mathematics being used to support A level science subjects. This latter combination was confirmed by our research and we found nothing to suggest that in the three years since the HMI review this pattern has begun to change.

AS levels in modern languages were, however, mentioned in a number of schools as being successful in a way that other AS subjects were not. National entry figures for 1994 indicate that one in ten AS entries were in modern languages compared to approximately one in 15 entries at A level. This relative success in a 'niche market' was attributed to the qualitative difference of the AS level from the A level in some boards (with no examination of literary study nor written language) and reflects the increasing acceptance of the importance of modern languages and their service subject status. At a much lower level of take-up, a parallel can be seen in the role of information technology and computing syllabuses.

An intermediate qualification?

One role not intended for AS levels when they were launched is that of an intermediate examination. In a very few isolated cases schools, while understanding the intention behind AS levels, had seen in the examination the possibilities of an intermediate academic qualification, teaching the whole AS syllabus in one year with assessment at 17+. Given the original purpose of the AS this is a practice which has been heavily criticised by HMI (HMI, 1992) though in these schools and in others there was a feeling that there was a real need for an academic qualification at an intermediate level. Three distinct but related reasons were put forward in interviews with teachers and students.

First, it was felt there was a need for an intermediate qualification for those students who were not yet ready to tackle a two year A level course. As we shall see in Chapter 7 there is a parallel here with students for whom it is appropriate to take an intermediate level GNVQ before embarking on the GNVQ advanced level. In both cases there are clear implications for the funding of three year sixth form courses if this should become standard practice for a significant number of students.

Second, heads of sixth form identified the desirability of providing a medium for the certification of achievement for those who leave after one year of an A level course as discussed in Chapter 3 in respect of modular Advanced level courses. This, of course, would involve the careful sequencing of modules of different levels as well as separate certification with credit banking and the opportunity for future transferability.

The third reason advanced was the provision of a general education qualification between GCSE and A level for those who did not wish to undertake a vocationally-based course but who sought further study. In many schools the only option for students was GCSE courses, either as re-takes or new subjects. This GCSE route was generally not considered to be at all appropriate though it remains relatively popular with 11 per cent of post-16 full-time students re-taking GCSEs (Stanton, 1994, p244). Nevertheless a number of schools had been obliged by funding constraints and the desire to develop vocational courses to cut back on the range and/or timetable time of their GCSE courses or to cease to offer the one year GCSE re-take route. As one head of sixth form explained:

In 1991 (we) began to look very critically at post-16 provision, if we wanted to expand some courses had to cut back on others, so we pruned ad hoc provision of GCSE back to a sensible package of five or six, so that we can afford vocational provision at Intermediate level.

If AS and GCSE were seen by heads of sixth form as inappropriate for meeting the perceived need for an intermediate academic qualification, were schools looking to new post-GCSE qualifications such as the NEAB's pilot Certificate of Extended Studies or 'E level' situated part-way between GCSE and A level or the AEB's Certificate of Further Studies (CFS) being an alternative to GCSE resits?

Both of the independent schools in the 20 schools visited in the research project were offering an E level subject. One school was entering the Year 11 top set for E level Mathematics instead of Additional Maths, the other was experimenting with E level French to give a qualification at the end of Year 12 for prospective Year 13 AS level candidates. As with AS level both institutions stressed the importance of universities recognising E level as a useful qualification. It was also felt important for the syllabuses to be compatible with Advanced level syllabuses. There was, however, little evidence in the schools in our research that the CFS qualification was being used. One school was entering students on the one year sixth GCSE courses for Sports Studies and two schools reported an interest, though no definite intention, to offer CFS subjects.

An extension of the intermediate qualification role could be seen in some schools where there was a certain amount of movement between A and AS level, and in both directions. Some students had begun AS courses and moved to A level though this was less common than those who had 'dropped down to AS level'. The use of this phrase by a number of teachers seemed to imply a difference in levels though some reservation was expressed by the same teachers that AS was not a course for weak students and that it was equally as demanding as a full A level course. One head of sixth form explained:

> In this school AS is seen as for youngsters who cannot cope with A levels, it's as simple as that. If a youngster cannot cope with a full A level course, we cut the workload, put them onto an AS course, they might be able to get something out of that rather than failing the A level course.

Impediments to the uptake of AS levels

A major difficulty with AS levels has been the size of the syllabuses which though intended to be half that of an A level are widely perceived as being disproportionately large. In the original consultation document (DES, 1984) and in their public presentation (DES, 1986) the expectation was clear that a major pattern of the use of AS would be to replace the study of one A level by two AS levels. A statement from the Standing Conference on University Entrance emphasised:

> Universities strongly believe in the importance of broadening the curriculum and intend to incorporate AS levels into their admissions procedures. For most courses a combination of two A levels and two AS levels will be regarded as equivalent to three A levels.

(DES, 1986, p5)

Original fears in some of the schools that universities would not value AS level had not been confirmed and the research found no suggestion that Higher Education institutions were discriminating against students with AS. However, the clear view of teachers and students was that study for two AS levels involves significantly more work than that for one A level and that thus it was harder to gain the same number of points for entry to HE. This was felt to be not only because the content of an AS syllabus was more than half that of an A level syllabus but also because the study of two subjects was more demanding in itself. The position was summed up by one head of sixth form thus:

> The impression is that they (AS levels) are more than half A level and therefore 2+2 is a greater workload than three A levels and a lot of youngsters at the moment are under pressure. Could have 3+1, but limited to very high ability who are prepared to put in a lot of work. But to be more acceptable they need to be rationalised so that they are half or less than half. The positive experience of AS is where students doing three sciences have picked up an AS in Modern Languages, very high ability again, or doing three sciences and picking up AS Maths, for medicine, an enormous workload.

The perceived size of the AS syllabuses is related to timetabling issues and the cause of one school's reluctance to go down the route of AS:

> Each head of department was asked to come along (to the meeting) having looked at the AS level in their particular subject. I think that most people felt there was a lot more than half a syllabus within the AS. And with a number of people, all together, saying really they didn't feel as happy about taking the AS as they did with the A level syllabus because of the syllabus part of it and also because they wouldn't have liked to offer an AS instead of the A level...and we don't have the staffing to be able to offer that alongside the A levels that we offer at present.

Schools thus faced a dilemma with regard to the timetabling of AS courses. Several schools wished to offer more AS levels but found that it was not ideal to co-teach A and AS level courses and yet did not have the staffing resources to allow them to run separate AS groups for very small numbers of students. The design of many AS syllabuses simply did not permit effective co-teaching though where the AS syllabus content was a subset of the A level syllabus fewer problems were found.

While the generally low levels of enthusiasm for AS levels in schools can partly be explained by the internal factors discussed above, a number of interviewees picked up the point made obliquely by HMI that the role of AS levels wasn't fully understood. The view which came across was not that the intended role of AS levels was not recognised or appreciated but rather that some schools did not accept that AS could fulfil this role. They felt that AS was simply trying to achieve the same as A level but in more subject areas. It was seen as questionable whether this was the type of breadth that was needed and that even if it was how did adding a fourth subject really make a significant difference? A further point raised was that the AS levels had nothing to offer those pupils for whom A level was in any case too hard.

Regeneration of AS levels?

In September 1993 the Secretary of State for Education, John Patten, wrote to SCAA to reaffirm the government's commitment to AS levels and to seek advice on the 'remaining obstacles' to the take-up of AS levels particularly with regard to concerns about the size of the AS syllabuses and timetabling difficulties (*DfE News* 376/93). The response based on a consultation on AS levels was largely positive and in 1995 SCAA sought to reinforce the position of AS levels by publishing *Using the Advanced Supplementary Examination* (SCAA, 1995). This practical booklet provided guidance and information on the ways that AS levels could be and were being used in schools and colleges. What it did not offer though were revisions to the A and AS system.

What then could be done to make AS levels more attractive as a means of broadening the curriculum or is it the case that the government is flogging a dead horse? While a minority of heads of sixth form clearly believed that AS levels had no future, a good number remained committed to them but were looking to SCAA to implement a number of changes to syllabus size and to the relationship with A level. Some, however, believed a further step to adjust the level of AS examinations to an intermediate level would be necessary. Two sixth form heads took an opposite stance, arguing that what was required was not watered down versions of A level syllabuses but the provision of distinctive AS syllabuses designed to offer a different approach to the A level by making the subject study more interesting for non-specialists. While this could make the syllabuses more suitable for broadening the academic curriculum, any such developments would of course preclude co-teaching and need additional staffing. A number of interviewees made the point that there was a need for re-education about AS levels in their schools. One commented:

> AS is seen to be a bolt-on to the mainstream traditional curriculum and conservative attitudes among students and parents have often meant they have stayed with what has been known. The lack of take-up has increased people's wariness. Within our school the few AS subjects offered reinforces the idea that it is peripheral. We need a bigger shift all through school over preceding years to having a broader view of the post-16 curriculum. Students are coming up thinking in terms of

narrowing down still further and to encourage them to take at least four subjects in a sense goes against the grain of their thinking and expectations. While universities have made positive statements about AS you only need one or two statements to the contrary that it sows those seeds of doubt, becomes out of proportion to what the overall actual picture is.

On the positive side, the development of new subject cores has had the benefit of defining common ground between A and AS syllabuses to facilitate co-teaching. Equally quasi-modularisation (through units, papers or modules) has gone some way to ensuring that the weighting of AS (e.g. three modules) is half that of the equivalent A level syllabus (six modules). In theory students are thus able to complete the modules for the AS levels in Year 12 before deciding whether to continue in that subject to A level in Year 12 or use the time released for another purpose. This was a model that several schools were considering or had started using, though the timetabling was not as straightforward as it might seem.

The experience of one school offering AS with modular A levels had been that students wanted to do AS in one year but that the staff had found this hard to reconcile with the A level syllabus and the order in which they wanted to teach the modules. Another school teaching modular AS over two years had found that as the pattern of the required A level modules varied throughout the year the intensity of study varied from eight periods per week to no periods in that subject. This AS study had therefore occupied a student's full A level subject block over two years. These timetabling problems were not considered to be insurmountable but did indicate the need for careful planning and scheduling of modules within subjects.

A modular route to breadth?

In the 16–19 review led by Sir Ron Dearing one of the supplementary questions asked by the Secretary for State was how curriculum breadth could be achieved. In addition to the development of core skills in the academic curriculum, Dearing undertook a consideration of: 'the case for reformulating the present AS examination, so that instead of covering half an A level syllabus in depth, it would cover the syllabus content in the breadth and depth appropriate for one year's study' (Dearing, 1995, para. 14.11).

The revised form of the AS would then be that of an intermediate 17+

examination with many of the advantages expressed above. Its role in broadening the curriculum would be further strengthened by the introduction of an enhanced version of a national advanced certificate which, by way of illustration, would record achievement: 'in five subjects, with at least two at the full A level standard (and above a specified grade) and the others in the reformulated AS level, together with the three core skills mandatory in GNVQ' (ibid., para. 14.12).

The A and AS achievement accredited thus would not be dissimilar in many aspects from that envisaged in the N and F proposals of the Schools Council.

The problems of syllabus size, co-teachability and the perception of AS as standing outside of the A level system may thus find a solution in the emerging qualifications framework of the academic and vocational curricula. The rationalisation of A and AS level subject syllabuses through the development of new subject cores together with the expansion of availability and take-up of modular syllabuses has already begun to result in a system which could support AS as a route to subject breadth. Dearing's proposals for an enhanced national certificate at advanced level, if realised, offer the opportunity for a formal high-level recognition of broad achievement coupled with specialist study.

Whereas the government's public face has been set against the accreditation and credit transfer of individual modules, several revised GCE Advanced level syllabus schemes based on subject cores are using AS to accredit combinations of modules or papers and to combine AS and A level in multiple awards. An extension of accreditation to smaller groups of GNVQ units would allow AS to be used as the basic unit for credit accumulation and transfer within a wider framework incorporating vocational programmes. This would be in line with the scheme envisaged at the time of the development of the draft principles by SEAC's working party on A/AS interrelationships which considered that the role of AS in broadening the curriculum would only be fulfilled if AS became the basic unit of study:

> AS courses need to be seen to embody the advanced level standard and to be available in a wide range of subjects/subject areas. A level examinations, however, may be available in a smaller number of subjects/subject areas than at present. This arrangement of AS and A examination courses would enable students more readily to assemble a broad study programme since the unit of study would be one sixth of the normal full-time programme rather than one third.
>
> (SEAC, 1991, p11)

The major advantage of using AS as the basic unit of credit

accumulation and transfer, apart from the fact that it is already recognised by SCAA and the examination boards for accreditation at an agreed level and weighting, would be that this would circumvent the problems of the variety of assessment formats and different weightings of modules, units and papers. The AS, rather than the A level's constituent modules or papers, thus has the potential to become a unit of accreditation as part of the framework linking the vocational and academic curricula.

How successfully A level examination boards and syllabus developers will be able to work towards a common weighting for A and AS level papers, units and modules that corresponds to the vocational qualifications framework remains to be seen. What is certain is that this would not have been the intention of the former Department for Education as was stated by the Further and Higher Education Minister in his speech to the Northern Examinations and Assessment Board's conference on the future of A levels: 'let me make absolutely clear that modular GCE syllabuses are not intended to be, and must not become, a step towards a single qualifications system' (Boswell, 1994, p7). With the establishment of the Department for Education and Employment to oversee the development of both academic and vocational post-16 curricula the mood has shifted towards a more integrative approach to post-compulsory education and training and concerted attempts are being made to bring in a coherent system and one that will build in greater breadth.

CHAPTER 5

The Background to the Vocational Curriculum

Assessment frameworks

It has been said that 'vocational students were at the heart of the colleges of further education' (Hall, 1994, p47) and this applies equally to the vocational curriculum. Since the nineteenth century, examining bodies such as the City and Guilds of London Institute and the Royal Society of Arts have set standards for and made awards to successful students attending day and evening classes in a very wide range of technical subjects. The City and Guilds was founded in 1878 by the livery companies in the City and has grown into one of the world's largest examining bodies. It does not run its own courses, but examines around 500,000 candidates in nearly 300 different vocational areas (Hall, 1994, p54) at a very wide range of levels from pre-vocational 14–16 year old schoolchildren to senior managers in industry. The Royal Society of Arts commenced examining in 1856, and, through its Examination Board, remains the largest provider of qualifications for those entering and working in office-based occupations. An important new body evolved in this area in 1983 when the Business Education Council (BEC) merged with the Technician Education Council (TEC) to form BTEC, the Business and Technician (now Technology) Education Council. This controls a large range of awards for industry, agriculture, business, public administration, leisure services, information technology and employment in caring. Members of the Council are appointed directly by the Secretary of State for Education and they normally reflect the interests of the areas of employment in which BTEC makes awards. BTEC does not run courses and it does not set examinations. It is in essence a validating body which, after checking that staffing and resources are suitable, approves centres to run and assess their own courses. BTEC then provides guidance and monitors standards through its well established quality control mechanisms. Following a long tradition in further education, the awards made by BTEC are normally either diplomas for full-time study or equivalent certificates for part-time students. For young people in the age range 16–19 years there are essentially two levels – First and National. Highers are also available, but these are classified as higher education. They are commonly taught in many further education colleges and in some universities, but they are normally obtained by students who on completion of their courses are over 19 years of age. Registrations for BTEC First and National awards grew significantly through the 1980s, and by the end of the decade it is fair to claim that they formed the heart of the curriculum of most further education colleges. In particular BTEC Nationals in many fields were well regarded qualifications not only for employment but also for entry to higher education. Many polytechnics (soon to be renamed universities) were prepared to admit students with BTEC Nationals to their courses, and, although this was less common in the traditional pre-1992 universities, it was by no means unknown.

In the 1980s there was increasing concern at the Manpower Services Commission (MSC), which operated under the auspices of the Department of Employment, about what was often called the 'vocational qualifications jungle'. In the mid 1980s there were five major national examining bodies and six regional bodies in this field. There were, in addition, about 250 professional bodies and about 120 industrial training organisations all engaged in accrediting and/or examining their own awards. In total thousands of different qualifications were available which were largely unrelated and which were not required to fit into any kind of overall national framework. It was difficult for specialists and impossible for ordinary citizens, young and old, to see their way through these complex structures which were fairly described as a 'jungle'. Pressures from within the MSC and the Department of Employment, which need to be more fully investigated, led to the setting up of a Review of Vocational Qualifications (RVQ) in 1985. This took place under the auspices of the MSC and the DES and the Working Group was chaired by the industrialist, Oscar De Ville. Its main recommendation was the setting up of the National Council for Vocational Qualifications (NCVQ) which came into existence in 1986. NCVQ's main functions were and are 'to promote, develop, implement and monitor a comprehensive system of vocational qualifications throughout the United Kingdom (excluding Scotland)' (NCVQ, 1994, p26) and its sponsoring departments are the Department for Education and Employment (DFEE), the Welsh Office and the Northern Ireland Office. NCVQ neither examines nor awards qualifications itself, but performs a quality control function. It has powers to regulate and awarding bodies in the vocational area need its stamp of approval. NCVQ requires that a 'lead body' on which employers are strongly represented, is set up for each occupational sector. The lead body is charged with specifying in some detail the standards of competence required by NVQs at different levels in its sector. RVQ also proposed that NCVQ should also be given the task of organising and ordering the hundreds of qualifications on offer. NCVQ has divided qualifications into a framework of five hierarchical levels which denote different standards. These levels and their descriptors (NCVQ, 1992, p12) are given below.

The NVQ Framework

Level 1: competence in the performance of a range of varied work activities, most of which may be routine and predictable.

Level 2: competence in a significant range of varied work activities, performed in a variety of contexts. Some of the activities are complex and non-routine, and there is some individual responsibility or autonomy. Collaboration with others, perhaps through membership of a work group or team, may often be a requirement.

Level 3: competence in a broad range of varied work activities performed in a wide variety of contexts and most of which are complex and non-routine. There is considerable responsibility and autonomy, and control or guidance of others is often required.

Level 4: competence in a broad range of complex, technical or professional work activities performed in a wide variety of contexts and with a substantial degree of personal responsibility and autonomy. Responsibility for the work of others and the allocations of resources is often present.

Level 5: competence which involves the application of a significant range of fundamental principles and complex techniques across a wide and often unpredictable variety of contexts. Very substantial personal autonomy and often significant responsibility for the work of others and for the allocations of substantial resources feature strongly, as do personal accountabilities for analysis and diagnosis, design, planning, execution and evaluation.

As the above shows, NVQs, unlike some traditional qualifications, are designed to test competences and outcomes normally seen in terms of abilities to perform specific tasks and do certain jobs (Spours, 1991). They are divided into units which can be accumulated at the candidate's own pace. The NVQ system was introduced primarily to try to raise the standard of people's competence at work and its applicability extends well beyond the 16–19 age range. Although NVQ Levels 4 and 5 are normally too advanced for 16 to 19 year olds, it will be seen later in this chapter how the NCVQ and its work has made a considerable impact on the education and training of this age range in the 1990s. Even in the late 1980s NVQs were used to some extent, but probably with more limited success than had been initially hoped, to accredit young people's placements and achievements on the Government's Youth Training programme. NVQs always require work-based experience, and, although they are sometimes taken in further education colleges and occasionally even in schools, their overall impact on the training of 16 to 19 year olds has remained relatively, and, some might argue, disappointingly small. It was the advent of GNVQs, which were piloted in 1992 and became generally available in 1993, which transformed this situation, and it was in this way that NCVQ was put into a central position in the education and training of 16 to 19 year olds. This important development will be considered in detail later in this chapter.

Developing vocational courses in colleges and schools from the 1970s to the early 1980s

By the 1970s it was clear that for a variety of reasons a significant number of 16 year olds wanted a further year of full-time education after the minimum leaving age. These young people were often uninterested in and unsuitable for A level courses. Many of them were also unsure about their future career aspirations which meant that the existing job-specific vocational courses available in the further education colleges did not meet their needs either. At first colleges and schools tried to accommodate the increasing number of such students by fitting them into existing provisions such as re-sit GCE Ordinary (O) levels. Such a diet proved unsatisfactory for the majority of these students. They found repeating material which they had already failed in Year 11 boring and soul-destroying and understandably, the failure rate for re-sit O levels was high. Teachers and lecturers increasingly took the view that these students should be encouraged to look forward to and prepare for the world of work after school and college rather than go back over the failings of an unsuccessful time in Years 10 and 11.

In schools a new Certificate of Extended Education (CEE) was introduced. This was school subject based and students were assessed in five subjects at the age of 17. Schools had considerable freedom over syllabus content and methods of assessment and they were able to adapt subjects to meet the particular needs of their own pupils. Content was often made relevant to the world of work and vocational elements introduced as appropriate. At the same time rather different developments were taking place in the further education sector. City and Guilds began to offer courses that were much more specifically pre-vocational in their orientation than CEE. City and Guilds foundation courses, which were focused on groups of related industries, aimed at helping students make more informed vocational choices. A general vocational preparation course also launched by City and Guilds also proved particularly popular. The Royal Society of Arts entered the field with general pre-employment courses for office work, and in skills required in personal services and the distributive trades. These courses were taken up in schools as well as colleges with City and Guild's general course making the greatest inroads. Often link courses between schools and some of the more specialised departments in further education such as building or catering were established so that pupils could gain access to the specialist equipment and staff located there. Pupils and students were increasingly involved in periods of work experience.

At the end of the 1970s the developments in CEE and the FE pre-vocational courses were reviewed in separate official reports. It was agreed that there was an urgent need for new provisions for 16 to 17 year olds of average and less than average abilities, and that courses for this group should be vocationally orientated, helping them 'to understand what employers would expect from them and what they should expect from employment'. The school-focused report recommended the continuation of CEE on the basis of individual subjects with assessment by examination. The FE report, entitled *A Basis for Choice* (FEU, 1979), favoured a common core of vocational preparation with profile assessment and records of achievement rather than examinations. It did not want subject components and proposed a core curriculum 'framework' or 'structure' of pre-vocational studies. Eventually the Government opted for the FE report, *A Basis for Choice,* which proved to be a most influential document. From this a new course and qualification, the Certificate of Pre-vocational Education (CPVE) was developed in the mid 1980s. It was available in both colleges and schools and formed an important part of the Government's training strategy.

When it was launched, it was given wide publicity and strong support from ministerial level.

As originally envisaged (DES, 1982) CPVE was to form a full-time counterpart to the Youth Training Scheme and it was expected that the aspirations of CPVE and YTS candidates, although not identical, would overlap. The target group of young people for CPVE was initially defined more in terms of those who were to be excluded than included. The Government indicated that CPVE was not to cater for those (i) who had the potential to take two or more A levels, (ii) who had clear vocational objectives in mind, (iii) who were better advised to try to improve their existing O level or CSE qualifications and (iv) who still required remedial help in basic subjects. It was expected that CPVE would meet the needs of about 80,000 young people per annum although the Government saw the number of potential candidates as at least twice this figure.

During the early planning stage the Government talked in relatively conventional terms about developing CPVE syllabuses and their potential content. Later, when CPVE ultimately emerged, it was defined, rather like *A Basis for Choice*, as a course framework and did not prescribe detailed syllabus content. The CPVE framework included a common core which was needed in adult life and which would be applied in a variety of employment situations. In addition, students were helped and required to develop their interests and skills in one or more of five specified vocational areas. All schemes were required to include at least 15 days' work experience, and assessment was based on 'a continuous collection of statements about a student's competence'. Individual counselling and guidance formed an important part of the course, and there was an expectation of considerable discussion and negotiation between student and tutor concerning the individual's programme of work. During the course CPVE students build up portfolios of work, and profiles were kept which contained information about achievements, competences and capabilities. There was often considerable emphasis on job seeking and enterprise skills, and sometimes students were involved in setting up and running their own mini-businesses. For some years CPVE was controlled by a Joint Board for Pre-Vocational Education set up by BTEC and CGLI. By the mid 1980s the Government had in place two new education and training schemes for 16 year olds. Firstly, there was the YTS which was largely based in the workplace, and, secondly, there was CPVE available normally on a full-time basis in schools and colleges. Both were vocational preparation schemes, and owed much to pioneering work undertaken in the MSC which at this time was at the height of its influence. It was an irony, not unnoticed by many teachers and lecturers, that it was during a period of very high youth unemployment that more stress than ever before had been placed on pre-vocational education and training. There can be little doubt, however, that CPVE represented a major innovation in curriculum planning, teaching and learning styles and assessment strategies (Macintosh, 1986, p89).

The place of CPVE in the vocational curriculum was soon beset by problems (Spours, 1991). Almost as soon as CPVE had been introduced under the Joint Board, BTEC decided to offer its own First Diploma. This operated from 1986 and was available in further education colleges, but initially the Government did not permit it to be offered in schools. The BTEC First Diploma was more vocationally specific and had less emphasis on the pre-vocational than CPVE. In colleges BTEC First provided a clear and obvious progression route into the more advanced and well regarded BTEC National Diploma courses. Almost immediately CPVE and BTEC Firsts were placed in a highly competitive position in the further education sector, and there is little doubt that lecturers often, even normally, advised the more able of the 16 year olds in the original target group to choose the BTEC First rather than the CPVE. With RVQ and the setting up of NCVQ the problems for CPVE were exacerbated. As a pre-vocational course, CPVE did not sit easily within the hierarchical framework for vocational qualifications which NCVQ was beginning to develop. Although some attempts at accommodation were made in 1987, it remained clear that CPVE did not fit well with the new structures. Numbers of students on CPVE courses were well short of those originally envisaged by the Government, and from 1987/8 they began to fall with the reduction being particularly marked in the further education sector where BTEC Firsts were preferred.

Evaluations and inspectors' reports soon began to highlight further difficulties for the CPVE. It was felt that employers neither understood nor valued it. There were doubts about rigour and consistency of practice across different centres. It was sometimes alleged that students in some schools and colleges were required to produce extensive, well researched and well presented portfolios while others were getting away with comparatively brief and at times rather scrappy notes. Exceptional achievement on the CPVE was not always differentiated sufficiently clearly enough from basic minimum completion level. The issue of progression from the CPVE tended to become more, rather than less, serious. In practice it proved particularly difficult to move from CPVE to BTEC National courses. Although most further education colleges were familiar with CPVE students, they often demanded four GCSEs at grade

C or above or a BTEC First for entry to a BTEC National course. At the end of their CPVE, many students found that they were offered places not on BTEC National courses but on BTEC Firsts only. This was widely regarded as unsatisfactory for both students and their teachers. Some students were disillusioned, feeling that their year on the CPVE had taken them nowhere; while many further education staff believed strongly that a basic or ordinary performance on the CPVE was an inadequate preparation for a BTEC National. Increasingly in practice the target group of students for CPVE was modified. By the end of the 1980s CPVE catered mainly for a relatively narrow range of low ability students. This was particularly so in further education where some colleges had begun to use the CPVE for students with learning or language difficulties (Hall, 1994). As this happened the status of the CPVE declined even further in the eyes of students, their parents and employers. In an hierarchical society such as England CPVE was soon perceived as a course for the less able, and as such unsuitable to meet the needs of middle range vocational students.

In the Summer of 1990 BTEC made a decisive entrepreneurial move, proposing that the Government should permit schools to offer its First Diplomas. Tim Eggar, Minister of State for Education, announced in December that he had been persuaded and that schools should be enabled to put on BTEC Firsts from September 1991. It is clear from official correspondence that the Government was concerned about CPVE's progression problems and by this time regarded the BTEC First as a better qualification than CPVE. There seemed to be little understanding of the fact that BTEC First Diplomas were vocational qualifications and that CPVE was pre-vocational intended for the, as yet, vocationally uncommitted. John Sellars, BTEC's chief executive, acknowledged that many schools would lack, at least initially, the specialised accommodation, equipment and staffing to launch these courses, but he hoped that neighbouring further education colleges would help out as far as they could. Schools had been allowed to offer BTEC Nationals for some years, but very few (about 30) did so and their offerings were largely restricted to business and design. It is difficult to imagine that BTEC and the Government had not realised the consequences for CPVE of a widespread take-up of BTEC Firsts in schools and sixth form colleges. At the same time Eggar asked BTEC and CGLI to dismantle the Joint Board for CPVE. CGLI was requested to take sole responsibility for CPVE which it was told to revamp in several respects including rigour, assessment and progression. CGLI quickly agreed to do this, and Susan Fifer headed the unit which took charge of the necessary developments.

Early in 1991 she produced the first drafts of what eventually became the DVE, the successor to CPVE. Some radical modifications were planned and CPVE's approach of a common core with a vocational focus now became the more occupationally specific DVE with opportunities to develop core skills. Steps were also to be taken in accrediting centres to make sure that the new course was not to be used almost exclusively for small groups of largely low ability students – a problem which had beset CPVE. The question of how DVE could be used by young people to obtain credits towards other qualifications such as NVQs was also considered.

As all this was taking place, the Government's proposals to introduce GNVQs were published in Education and Training for the 21st Century (DES/DOE/Welsh Office, 1991). There is little evidence to suggest that those working on the DVE at CGLI were given much advanced warning of this. Eventually the DVE with a three level framework (Foundation for the age range 14 to 16 years; Intermediate for a one year post-16 course; and National for a two year post-16 course) was approved by Eggar in June 1991. In many ways the new DVE had been overtaken by events, particularly the recently invented GNVQs, and the highest level (National) of the DVE was never developed. Increasingly CGLI, like BTEC and the RSA Examination Board, had to concentrate its efforts on the emerging GNVQs. Some of those concerned with the development of DVE hoped and, to some extent, initially expected that it would be possible to incorporate the Diploma into the GNVQ framework. Within a few months it became clear that this was out of the question and that the two structures would have to remain entirely separate. It is not easy to understand why the Government agreed to allow BTEC First Diplomas to be delivered in schools and asked CGLI to develop the DVE when it was within six months to launch a completely new framework for school and college based vocational qualifications itself. A number of schools found themselves in the difficult, expensive and time consuming business of converting from CPVE to BTEC Firsts or to DVE and then immediately having to change again to GNVQ Intermediates. The teachers affected by these rapid and unpredictable changes in direction were understandably both tired and disillusioned. They found the pace of change imposed on them unreasonable and were often convinced that these, perhaps desirable, developments could and should have been better planned and managed to the highest level. In the mid 1990s the DVE continues to exist, but now serves largely the needs of 14 to 16 year olds. Early in 1995 there were almost 27,000 candidates registered for Foundation DVE at about 450 centres (figures supplied by CGLI). For

Intermediate level (one year post-16) there were only about 6,900 candidates registered at 260 centres. In the 16 to 19 age range DVE has now been totally eclipsed by GNVQ.

Further initiatives in the vocational and technical curriculum

Throughout this century several attempts have been made in this country to develop new categories of schools whose primary and defining characteristic is a specific technical or vocational curriculum. There is an excellent analysis of these developments in Michael Sanderson's book, *The Missing Stratum: Technical School Education in England, 1900–1990s* (Sanderson, 1994) and other authors such as Gary McCulloch (McCulloch, 1989) have discussed similar themes. Sanderson has shown that when and where technical schools were set up, they were well regarded and much appreciated by staff, pupils, parents and employers. They were able to recount many success stories of pupils from humble origins who later in life achieved highly in industry and commerce. On the other hand, many large industrialists, leading educationalists and senior politicians from both major political parties remained unenthusiastic even sceptical of them, and, in the long term, failed to give them the necessary political and financial support for their survival. For most of the twentieth century technical schools were not expected, even permitted, to develop sixth forms which were still regarded as the preserves of the grammar schools. Consequently their impact on the 16–19 curriculum in schools was minimal. When a small number of grammar schools attempted to develop an alternative vocational curriculum for a proportion of their pupils in the 1930s, they were vigorously opposed by the Board of Education and ultimately required to drop such experiments. In much more recent times city technology colleges with a specific mission to develop vocational curricula have been set up, and in 1992/93 the 'Technology Colleges Initiative' with rather similar aims was introduced. It is still too early to assess what impact these innovations will make on the 16–19 vocational curriculum, although the very restricted number of City Technology Colleges makes it unlikely that they will have much effect on a national scale. Initially only grant maintained and voluntary aided schools were eligible to apply for grants under the 'Technology Colleges Initiative', but this has now been extended to all secondary schools. With considerable cash incentives available, relatively large numbers of schools are becoming involved or showing interest in this scheme which may in the long term prove to be an innovation of considerable importance.

There is little doubt that the major national innovation in the curriculum in the 1980s prior to the passing of the Education Reform Act of 1988 was TVEI which was announced by the Prime Minister in 1982. TVEI was administered for some years by the Manpower Services Commission and later by the Training, Enterprise and Education Directorate (TEED) of the Department of Employment. Via TVEI considerable sums of money were made available to schools and colleges, when generally they felt very short of resources for development. These funds were provided to develop a new learning framework for the 14 to 18 age range irrespective of their abilities. After some initial scepticism in certain quarters, eventually all LEAs and nearly all maintained secondary schools and colleges became involved in the scheme – it proved impossible in the long term to ignore the considerable cash incentives. In TVEI emphasis was placed on preparing young people for the world of work, developing their problem-solving skills, their initiative, enterprise and motivation and generally encouraging more positive attitudes to employment in industry and commerce. It is impossible to generalise about the contents and methods of TVEI projects because they were so varied. Although further education was involved from the outset and the 16–18 curriculum was clearly part of TVEI's remit, available evidence suggests that many projects focused on 14–16 year olds in the first instance and only later considered the ramifications for post-16 students. There is broad consensus amongst those who have investigated TVEI that it impacted more strongly on the 14–16 age range than on the 16–19 curriculum. TVEI embraced neither qualifications nor examinations and was thus in a comparatively weak position in a sector of education so dominated by such phenomena. With such constraints its chances of making any real impact on either the academic–vocational divide in the 16–19 curriculum or even the 16–19 vocational curriculum itself were minimal.

The setting up of GNVQs

By the late 1980s it was clear that the new qualifications, NVQs, intended to transform the training of the workforce were not making the impact which the Government had hoped for and expected (Cross, 1991). The take-up of NVQs remained disappointingly small and NCVQ was criticised for the slow speed with which they were being put 'on stream'.

In 1989 a CBI Task Force chaired by Sir Bryan Nicholson, formerly chair of MSC, produced an influential report (CBI, 1989) which questioned whether NVQs in their existing form would be able to meet all the training needs of the nation. It called for the performance of NCVQ to be improved. The Task Force believed that there was still too much 'overly job-related training in employment which fails to lay the foundations for sufficient numbers of adaptive, flexible and responsive employees' (CBI, 1989, p13). NVQs were alleged to be too narrow for the development of flexible skills with NVQ units sometimes being concerned with isolated tasks in which the overall context was lost. Too much emphasis was placed on narrow, rather than broad based, competence with knowledge and skills relatively neglected. The CBI wanted common learning outcomes or core skills to be developed. It encouraged notions of broad 'generic' units of competence which were not to be set by the individual industry lead bodies, but occupational competences which were common to a wide range of jobs. The CBI Task Force was moving towards a new concept which, after further refinement, emerged as 'GNVQ'.

This same study raised the question of national attainment targets, pointing out that NVQs were much less well known and understood than academic qualifications such as A levels and GCSEs. It asserted that it was possible to look at broad comparisons between academic and vocational qualifications although it was acknowledged that there were difficulties in establishing rigorous equivalences (CBI, 1989). It went on to equate NVQ Level 2 with five GCSEs or better and NVQ Level 3 with a portfolio of two A levels plus five GCSEs. Since then Government has been very much involved in using, developing and publicising these ideas of equivalence between academic and vocational qualifications, but at no point have these notions been researched and systematically tested. From the outset they were asserted rather than investigated and established and this has continued.

At about the same time John Sellars, chief executive of BTEC, made much the same criticisms of NCVQ and NVQs as the CBI. He claimed that too many industry lead bodies were focusing on 'narrow, mechanistic, easily measurable competences' (*TES*, 20 October 1989) to the detriment of knowledge and intellectual content in many areas of education and training. He wanted to see more emphasis on personal effectiveness learning to broaden the curriculum and less on the narrow 'trade training' approach which he blamed on the 'evangelical zeal' of latecomers to the cause of employment relevance wanting simply to make their mark. In 1990 it became clear that BTEC would offer Level 3 NVQs, but these would not be recognised as BTEC National Diplomas or Certificates as such. Only those students who fully met the criteria for BTEC Nationals would be able to take these awards.

Although much of the evidence is not yet in the public domain, it is clear that by the second half of 1990 there was political demand for some major reorganisation at NCVQ. It is likely that this was initiated by Tim Eggar who had been appointed as Minister of State for Education and who had previous experience at the Department of Employment. Eggar knew of Sir Bryan Nicholson's successful chairing of the MSC and of his work on the CBI's Task Force which had been critical of both employers and the NCVQ in terms of the narrowness of NVQs. He hoped that Sir Bryan could be persuaded to take on the chair of NCVQ. Probably only after reassurances concerning future funding and powers for the Council were given, this was agreed. Meanwhile, the then director of NCVQ, Peter Thompson, had come out in favour of this country developing a worthwhile alternative to the 'academic fast track' to higher education. He wanted Britain to adopt a structure similar to Germany's dual system. In the past there had often been attempts to build bridges back to the academic fast track but these had only served to underline the second class status of the alternative route. Thompson proposed that the alternative should have distinctive aims and purposes of its own and that these should be based on the NVQ system. He concluded that 'a combination of A level/degree and NVQ routes is what is needed' (*Guardian*, 1 November 1990). Secretary of State, Kenneth Clarke, endorsed this approach early in 1991 and is reported to have come out in favour of 'broad-based NVQs assessed in ways suitable for use in full-time education' (*TES*, 29 March 1991). By this time Sir Bryan Nicholson had taken over as chair of NCVQ and, almost certainly at his instigation, Peter Reay, formerly of Cadbury Schweppes, was quickly appointed as its new chief executive.

Developments were now moving fast. By March 1991 it became public knowledge that NCVQ was developing a new set of qualifications, known as GNVQs, to be used in both further education colleges and schools. It was hoped that these would be ready to pilot from September 1992. GNVQs were to be offered at three levels and were to be alternatives to low grade GCSEs, good GCSEs and A levels. They were intended as preparation for practical vocational training or for higher education, and they were to be linked with broad occupational groups. They were to be assessed by project work and assignments rather than competences and were expected to be 'more like GCSE studies than straight vocational courses or conventional A levels' (*TES*, 29 March 1991). Criteria for GNVQs were to be drawn up by NCVQ rather than industry lead bodies, and it was expected that BTEC, CGLI and RSA would be the awarding bodies, although Gilbert Jessup, NCVQ's deputy director, indicated that school examining bodies might enter the field. Tim Eggar, who clearly took a lively interest in this area, stressed that GNVQs would have the same esteem as A levels. There can be little doubt that the catalyst for these developments was the appointment of Nicholson as chair of NCVQ. In his work for the CBI he had made it amply clear that he wanted to see vocational courses delivered in these ways and their place in the overall education and training system considerably strengthened. These ideas clearly appealed strongly to ministers such as Eggar, and it must be said that one person already working for NCVQ, Gilbert Jessup who had previously worked under Nicholson at the MSC, had already indicated that he wanted to see the NVQ outcome model extended and applied to as wide a spectrum of educational provision as possible (Jessup, 1991).

GNVQs were officially announced in May 1991 in the White Paper, *Education and Training for the 21st Century* (DES/DOE/Welsh Office, 1991). It was suggested there that:

> Many young people want to keep their career options open. They want to study for vocational qualifications which prepare them for a range of related occupations but do not limit their choices too early. Some want to keep open the possibility of moving on to higher education. Employers, too, want to have the opportunity of developing their young recruits' general skills, as well as their specific working skills. A range of qualifications is needed within the NVQ framework to meet these needs.

(ibid., p18).

GNVQs were to:

> Offer a broad preparation for employment as well as an accepted route to higher level qualifications, including higher education.

> Require the demonstration of a range of skills and the application of knowledge and understanding relevant to the related occupations.

> Be of equal standing with academic qualifications at the same level.

> Be clearly related to the occupationally specific NVQs, so that young people can progress quickly and effectively from one to the other.

> Be sufficiently distinctive from occupationally specific NVQs to ensure that there is no confusion between the two.

> Be suitable for use by full-time students in colleges, and, if appropriate in schools, who have limited opportunities to demonstrate competence in the workplace.

(ibid., p19)

Colleges, schools and awarding bodies were reminded rather pointedly that the Secretary of State had powers under section 24 of the 1988 Education Reform Act to regulate provisions for full-time students over the age of 16. It was announced that he would use these powers to require colleges and schools to offer only qualifications within the NVQ framework to students pursuing vocational options. It was acknowledged that this was to ensure that colleges and awarding bodies replaced older style vocational qualifications with NVQs (including GNVQs) as soon as possible. This requirement should be stressed because it was the means by which the Government could be absolutely certain that GNVQs would take a firm hold in the colleges. Even if they had reservations, BTEC and the colleges were given no option. They were being instructed to bring their existing courses into the NVQ or the GNVQ framework. For BTEC John Sellars expressed misgivings about this on many occasions as did staff and even students in the colleges. It was maintained that BTEC Nationals were well established and respected by staff, students and employers. They also provided a viable alternative route into higher education for some students. If this system was operating successfully, there seemed little reason to change it. There was certainly some feeling that the GNVQ framework was being imposed on a BTEC system which did not need it, and in 1992 Parry Rogers, chair of BTEC, accused NCVQ of 'leaning too heavily in favour of skills-based training at the expense of educational breadth' (*TES*, 6 November 1992). When some colleges and schools which had been accepted to pilot the new GNVQs indicated that they wished to retain their well tried and tested BTEC courses as a safety net, NCVQ told them that this was unacceptable. In the Summer of 1992 this led to withdrawals from the GNVQ pilots, but eventually NCVQ and BTEC came to an accommodation thus avoiding a long running dispute. In the new circumstances it is difficult to see how BTEC could have preserved its position. The NCVQ viewpoint was destined to prevail because it had strong political backing derived from the White Paper and the legislation itself. This whole exercise was, at least in part, about revitalising an ailing NVQ system and giving NCVQ a much more positive and central role in the control of mainstream full-time 16–19 education. Only with the advent of GNVQ did it become a major player in this field.

CHAPTER 6

Implementing the Vocational Curriculum in the 1990s

Putting GNVQs into practice

During the Summer of 1991 extensive effort was put into the planning and preparation of GNVQ. NCVQ set up a policy group which included representatives from a wide range of bodies with interests in the education and training area. The policy group produced a seminal document entitled *GNVQs: Proposals for the New Qualifications A Consultation Paper* (see Harrop, 1992, Appendix A, pp69–92), which was launched at a press conference on 8 October and went out to consultation during the Autumn of 1991. This paper set out the proposed criteria for GNVQs and in most respects established the basic characteristics of the qualification which have not been radically modified since. It was soon decided to pilot GNVQs at Levels 2 and 3 in five broad occupational areas: Leisure and Tourism; Manufacturing; Health and Care (later amended to Health and Social Care); Business and Administration (later amended to Business); Art and Design. Different working parties considered each of these areas.

From the outset parity of esteem and of standards between GNVQ Level 3 and A level was regarded as very important. This was, of course, a central concern of each of the working parties on the five occupational areas, but there was also some attempt made to match GNVQ structures to A levels by regulating the size of units. Level 3 GNVQs were to consist of 12 units and were to be equivalent to two A levels. Thus each GNVQ unit was to be comparable with one-sixth of an A level or one-third of an AS level. Such a structure offered potential for credit transfer between GNVQs and modular A levels.

It was not surprising that GNVQs were to incorporate core skills as by the early 1990s they were widely regarded as essential elements for vocational qualifications and there was increasing pressure to include them in academic qualifications as well. It was proposed that the delivery and assessment of core skills should be integrated into the whole programme. At this stage it was suggested that there should be five core skill areas: Communication; Numeracy (later Application of Number); Information Technology; Problem Solving and Personal Skills, but, because of certain later difficulties the last two were not made mandatory.

The issues which proved most difficult to resolve during the preparation of the consultation paper also generated the deepest differences of opinion in the consultation itself, and have continued to be the most controversial and intractable problems in the whole GNVQ area. They are largely concerned with assessment and grading. GNVQs were to be different from NVQs in a number of crucial respects. GNVQs were to assess skills, knowledge and understanding and would not 'seek to attest to occupational and professional competence' (Harrop, 1992, p75) as NVQs did. As Hyland has stressed, 'competence is rarely mentioned at all in the context of GNVQs' (Hyland, 1994, p107). The same author has argued that NVQs are essentially 'an exercise in accreditation' (*TES*, 20 September 1991), but from the outset it was acknowledged that GNVQs had to involve more than this as 'an understanding of the principles and processes which underlie competent performance in employment is considered to be a general feature of GNVQs' (Harrop, 1992, pp85–6). Such understanding was seen as crucial to 'generalisability' or 'the ability to transfer performance to the variety of situations a candidate might meet in the future' (Harrop, 1992, p86). According to the NCVQ consultation document it also formed 'the basis for future learning'. It was proposed that students should be assessed by projects and assignments in connection with each unit and that this assessment would be supplemented by written tests linked to each unit which would be centrally set and administered by the awarding bodies. It was felt that these tests should be externally set 'to achieve credible parity in relation to A levels' (Harrop, 1992, p86).

During 1991 there were clearly fears that the Government's insistence on the use of conventional examinations in nearly all GCSE and A level courses might be applied to GNVQs, but NCVQ successfully opposed this. There was strong support in the consultation for assessment by projects and assignments together forming a 'portfolio of evidence', but the question of externally set tests proved much more controversial with a majority against them. Two-thirds of the further education colleges consulted opposed them and a number pointed out that they were not part of current BTEC requirements which worked well. The Association of

Principals of Colleges believed that imposing external tests was 'to chase a mythical "academic respectability" and would be a retrograde step in education for vocation. It negates the philosophy of flexibility, accreditation of prior achievement and the assessment procedures for NVQs' (Harrop, 1992, pp37-8). BTEC was strongly against external tests, although CGLI and RSA believed they might be appropriate for some but not all units. Industry was quite divided in its response to this question.

Grading proved an equally contentious issue. There was some feeling that GNVQs, like NVQs, should not be graded at all as this went beyond the basic principle of reporting an attainment or competence. Others believed that parity of esteem and standards with A level could not be achieved without using grading particularly in relation to entry into higher education. Amongst those who supported grading there were differences between those who wished to see grading for individual units and those who favoured it only for the qualification as a whole. In the consultation a small majority came out for grading the whole without grading each unit. It is not easy to categorise views in this area. BTEC, which already graded units in its existing system, saw this as essential, but CGLI was opposed to it. Some in higher education positively supported grading and others regarded it as necessary if regrettable. There was a strong view that as long as A levels continued to be graded, admissions tutors would need similar yardsticks in the GNVQ area. It is clear that NCVQ staff were against the grading of course units, but acknowledged that high quality performance needed to be differentiated overall. It was eventually recommended that candidates would be awarded 'merit' and 'distinction' for appropriate levels of performance. Individual units were not to be graded separately, but merits and distinctions could be awarded on the overall quality of work presented in the portfolios of evidence. This decision was not supported by higher education with the Standing Conference on University Entrance comparing the proposal unfavourably with BTEC's existing practice (*TES*, 13 December 1991). It was claimed that admissions tutors would require more evidence of the quality of students' achievement than this provided. It has been argued that:

> In the development of GNVQs the vocational wheel has turned a full circle; with the abandonment of work-based competence, and the introduction of grading and externally set written tests, the NCVQ has moved about as far away from the basic foundational competence-based education and training procedures as it is possible to move while still retaining the NVQ label.
>
> (Hyland, 1994, p107)

It is a moot point whether it would have been better to change the label as well.

During the transitional period in which GNVQs were introduced there were inevitably, but frustratingly for those involved, some casualties. After long, very difficult and delicate negotiations on several fronts, one Yorkshire school known to the authors put in place in September 1992 a BTEC National in Business and Finance in conjunction with a neighbouring further education college. This course ran for only one year before it was overtaken by GNVQ. Eventually it had to be completely renegotiated and restructured to become a Level 3 GNVQ which, for particular local reasons, was operated under the auspices of a different awarding body. It proved very difficult to retain staff support and enthusiasm in such circumstances.

It was often in the further education colleges that there was reluctance to move from some of the more specialised BTEC Nationals to the wider, and some allege less focused, GNVQs. As John Pursaill of NCVQ has pointed out, initially it was not grasped 'that soon there were to be GNVQs, NVQs and nothing else' (Hyland, 1994, p116). The change to GNVQ was compulsory even if the new qualification was to be based primarily on the reworking and reconstitution of a BTEC course (Hyland, 1994, p107). Even in these circumstances the Government via NCVQ launched a major publicity campaign to promote GNVQs, and there was never any prospect that the new qualifications would be ignored. To crown this campaign and to ensure parity of esteem with their academic counterparts, Secretary of State, John Patten, announced that in future Level 3 GNVQs were to be known as 'vocational advanced or A levels'. Much less crucial in terms of publicity Level 2 GNVQs were named 'Intermediate' and Level 1 'Foundation'. Unlike other new qualifications such as AS levels which could be taken or left alone by institutions as they saw fit, GNVQs had their success virtually assured, not to say arranged, by Government sponsorship. Although secondary schools were able to ignore the vocational curriculum and GNVQs, if they so chose, in practice, further education colleges were obliged to embrace them from the outset – after all there could eventually be 'nothing else'. In essence the Government and NCVQ had put in place a core or national vocational curriculum for 16 to 19 year olds. Much as the schools had been required to follow the National Curriculum with 5 to 16 year olds from 1988, now the colleges and the school sixth forms had the vocational version for those students from the older age range who opted in the work-related direction. NCVQ was to do for vocational 16 to 19 education and training what the SCAA did for the academic curriculum in the schools.

Practice and experience in the schools

Evidence from our research in schools showed, not unexpectedly, wide variety of experience and practice in the vocational curriculum. At one extreme there were independent and grammar schools with no experience of the vocational curriculum at all and with no intention of changing that situation. A number of comprehensive schools, often situated in 'leafy lane' locations, had some but quite limited experience of vocational courses and were considering whether they should make the effort to enter this field with more vigour on a more extensive and planned basis. Several felt that they were being encouraged by Government to do so and seemed to be coming to the conclusion that this issue was urgent in terms of keeping up numbers and that they ought to move in this direction as soon as was practical. At the other extreme were a small number of often large comprehensives with a relatively long tradition, perhaps extending over fifteen years or more, of providing a vocational curriculum for a proportion of their students. These schools, and their numbers should not be exaggerated, often had staff in post with long and broad experience of teaching vocational courses and one school studied had the important asset of one key senior member of staff who had made significant contributions to national developments in this area. It was unsurprising that one or two such schools already had relatively extensive provisions in place by 1993/94 and were in a position to react swiftly to national developments. In the schools surveyed, in 1993/94 over twice as many students followed GNVQ Intermediate as GNVQ Advanced courses. Some schools indicated that they had consciously planned to build up their GNVQ provisions starting from Intermediate level. One GNVQ coordinator was at pains to stress how difficult Advanced GNVQs were and she doubted whether the students at her school would be able to cope with them. DVE, BTEC First and National Diplomas, the latter sometimes provided in conjunction with neighbouring further education colleges, were all well represented in the sample schools. Of the students on vocational courses 35 per cent were on Intermediate GNVQs, 15 per cent on Advanced GNVQs, 25 per cent on the DVE and 25 per cent on others (nearly all BTEC Diplomas).

Most of the schools had gained experience of vocational provisions through the CPVE in the 1980s. Quite a number of Leeds and Bradford schools still continued to hold the old CPVE course in high regard, stressing the virtues of its pre-vocational nature which allowed students to taste various kinds of vocational areas before commitment. They also believed that every student on it, regardless of ability level, obtained something positive from it. It is interesting to note that in an earlier survey for NCVQ John Pursaill also found that the CPVE/DVE was widespread and popular in Leeds (Harrop, 1992, p118). On the other hand, some schools, most of these situated in comparatively 'leafy lane' districts, expressed dissatisfaction with CPVE. It was said to lack credibility with local employers and parents and consequently attracted only a low take-up. In one 'middle-class' town parents and students opted for GCSE re-sits rather than CPVE which was loathed. Some schools criticised its lack of a specific vocational focus and suggested that, as far as the students were concerned, its purposes remained vague. From others there were allegations that it was insufficiently rigorous in its assessment procedures with little notion of national standards. Many schools stressed that CPVE's successors were considerably harder, but they supported this because they felt it helped to enhance the status and acceptability of vocational qualifications with employers, parents, higher education and students.

Considerable concern was expressed by many comprehensive schools that, since the demise of CPVE, there was a serious gap in suitable provision for the weakest students in the post-16 ability range and for those who were vocationally uncertain. Three schools which catered largely for students from inner city or large estates stressed that such provisions should not be seen exclusively in terms of preparation for employment, but were, at least in part, about building students' confidence and giving them a sense of achievement. There now seemed to be no courses which offered weak students the opportunity to taste and to sample. Schools found BTEC First and GNVQ Intermediate too difficult for these students and even DVE, like GNVQ, involved commitment to a particular vocational route. Some schools expected GNVQ Foundation to offer solutions in this area, but others believed that this would be both too vocationally committed and too difficult. One head of sixth form frankly admitted that he was in one sense relieved that his school was no longer catering for these kinds of students who were a 'considerable pain' and took up too much of his time, but, in another sense, he felt that they had every right to be part of a comprehensive school and should be supplied with suitable provisions. A school in a 'leafy lane' district found that the disappearance of CPVE had not led to the anticipated gap in provision because the new GNVQ courses were broad enough to cope with the vocationally uncommitted. In contrast one city school had been so concerned about the time lapse between the demise of CPVE and the arrival of Foundation GNVQ that it had devised its own basic vocational study scheme, which had recruited relatively well, to fill the gap.

Many schools brought out and stressed the strengths of vocational courses, particularly GNVQs. Their student-centred learning approaches were particularly appreciated as was their emphasis on continual assessment by coursework assignment and project rather than end of course conventional examinations. Schools felt that these factors, coupled with the notion that young people were being prepared to take up employment, aided student motivation considerably. These important positive considerations, however, should not mask the fact that there were also a number of negative attitudes which were strongly and commonly expressed.

There can be no doubt that many able students were generally sceptical of vocational courses, including GNVQs and they intended to continue to steer clear of them. Students from an independent school asserted that a stigma was attached to Advanced GNVQ and that it catered for the 'second rate', 'the thick' and 'those who could not cope with examinations'. Although in other schools feelings were expressed in less extreme terms; the judgements were essentially similar. Only in a small minority of institutions were notions that GNVQs were inferior to A levels questioned by students. In some schools A level students alleged that some of the students taken on to do GNVQ courses had poorer GCSE results than school admissions guidelines prescribed. In one school both students and staff expressed considerable, but pleasant, surprise when GNVQ students outperformed their A level counterparts in a public presentation at a business awareness event. Nearly all students reported that their teachers advised them to take A level courses if they were 'good enough'. Remarks such as, 'You'll get further with A levels, if you're intelligent enough to get an A at GCSE then you should be doing A level', were common. Some students felt that at least some of their teachers still believed that vocational courses were second rate – 'An awful lot of teachers still regard BTEC as second class and lots of pupils get the same idea, and it can put you down an awful lot on occasions'. Those students who were seen as aspiring realistically to university entrance were almost invariably directed towards the A level route. There was knowledge amongst secondary school students that Advanced GNVQs could provide entry to university, but some believed that 'better universities' preferred A levels.

A number of schools reported that very many parents in their areas still had to be persuaded of the value of vocational courses. Such parents wanted their children to do A levels even when they were clearly unsuitable in terms of abilities. In parents' eyes, vocational courses were frequently associated with further education colleges and were not regarded as proper activities for sixth forms. A relatively small minority of sixth form teachers also mentioned that their heads showed no real commitment to vocational courses and were very critical of the kinds of conduct and behaviour which they associated with students on such courses. They were only prepared to tolerate such students in their sixth forms because of the financial rewards brought to the school. A small number of heads of sixth form were frank enough to admit that they had developed vocational provisions mainly because they knew that they would lose students to competitor institutions if they did not.

The factors discussed in the previous paragraphs only underline how difficult it will be at the local level to achieve anything approaching parity of esteem between the academic and vocational routes. The latter is often lacking in clear definition in the minds of parents, students and even teachers, and insufficient distinction is sometimes drawn between different courses or different levels such as Advanced and Intermediate GNVQ. It is difficult to deny that teachers who tell students who obtained excellent GCSE results to do A levels rather than GNVQs are giving sensible, fair and good advice. It has to be admitted that GNVQs were not introduced to cater for these people, but for those who had fared rather less successfully. In these circumstances it was probably inappropriate for Government to have talked in terms of parity of esteem at all. As one deputy head commented: 'able kids are still suspicious of vocational courses, and it will take more than my lifetime to turn that around.'

Students made interesting comments about the extent to which they had received information about vocational provision in other institutions. Most felt that they were given basic information about courses in neighbouring colleges, but suggested that you had to take the initiative yourself if you wished to pursue such possibilities seriously. It was mentioned by both students and teachers that careers services often stressed college provisions strongly and in at least one case this emphasis rather annoyed sixth form staff. Several colleges and schools had negotiated their own joint arrangements for offering certain courses, and, although this clearly reduced any tensions in the short term, there was some evidence that these arrangements were proving unstable in a market climate. In some instances partner institutions seemed likely to pull out of joint arrangements and go their own separate ways. Several school teachers asserted that their students preferred the teaching provided in school to that given in the college. Some schools were adamant that they encouraged students to move to college in cases where that course of action was most appropriate. Others acknowledged that they needed to look after their own interests with respect to student numbers and did primarily promote their own sixth form provisions. There was comparatively little evidence of attempts to recruit potential sixth formers from neighbouring schools, although one grant maintained school acknowledged interest in attracting post-16 students from the local independent schools. Most students concluded that, although they were not pressurised to stay in their old schools for their sixth form courses, they were given every possible encouragement to do so with all the disadvantages of moving elsewhere often stressed. Two large comprehensive schools, with considerable experience of vocational work, expressed concerns about the pressures from market forces to expand into 'virtually everything like headless chickens' irrespective of a sound base and appropriate resourcing and staffing. This militated against sound provisions. One deputy head had a vision of city-wide cooperation between colleges and schools to achieve a planned high quality range of vocational courses available to all at convenient locations but regretted this could not happen in the current market-directed system.

The points made in the local survey concerning the early implementation of GNVQs largely echoed those being put forward nationally. There was widespread consensus that course documentation, and particularly its technical terms and its language, was inaccessible to both teachers and students. Many teachers complained how jargon-ridden it was. There was also considerable concern than GNVQ course literature was insufficiently specific and did not explain at all clearly how actual teaching programmes could and should be formulated. No sample assignments were provided. At the outset this situation was exacerbated because there were no suitable textbooks on the market. Teachers often felt on their own and in limbo. The school which was fortunate enough to have a member of staff with experience of the national developments in GNVQs used his broad expertise, asking him to talk other teachers through in their own language the requirements of the more difficult and opaque parts of the documentation. No other school in the survey had such an invaluable asset. Most schools made use of the INSET provisions on GNVQs available in their localities. There were some differences of opinion concerning the quality and utility of these provisions, but more reports were favourable than unfavourable. An issue which caused particular annoyance and resentment amongst some teachers was the requirement to become trained GNVQ assessors by taking NVQ units D32 and D33 and an additional unit, D34, to qualify as an internal verifier. These processes were seen as totally unnecessary for trained and experienced teachers, and were felt very strongly to be undermining professional standing. One teacher asserted that he simply refused to do this whatever the formal requirement, and teachers widely believed that they were being unfairly charged to demonstrate skills they already possessed.

National perspectives on the implementation of GNVQs

From 1992 GNVQs have increasingly dominated the vocational curriculum for 16 to 19 year olds at the national level. They have engendered both much enthusiasm and considerable criticism. It is now time to consider some of the latter.

It has sometimes been claimed that teachers were provided with insufficient guidance about what and how to teach on GNVQ programmes. Alan Smithers alleged that, despite the wishes of the awarding bodies, GNVQs had no syllabuses (Smithers, 1993), but other commentators, including NCVQ, have maintained that this was not so, only the language and layout were unconventional (*Education*, 25 February 1994). Some have argued that the performance criteria and range statements were quite explicit (*Education*, 10 June 1994), but it has also been reported that 'staff often commented on how little they knew in advance about course delivery, assessment requirements and methods etc' (FEU, Institute of Education and Nuffield Foundation, 1994, p22). OFSTED noted that methods of assessment and grading were 'inadequately developed and explained in the documentation and training' (OFSTED, 1994, p5), and stressed again and again that teachers were uncertain about the standards to be achieved. According to OFSTED, this demonstrated the need for much clearer and fuller course specifications which included knowledge content requirements, and for exemplar materials to be issued by NCVQ and the awarding bodies. Similar points were made by the Further Education Funding Council which added that the interpretation of NCVQ specifications had been more problematic for teachers who had not previously delivered vocational courses (FEFC, 1994b). Teachers found some of the performance criteria vague and some of the range statements too broad in scope to aid course design. Guidance about required content and standards were not always available from awarding bodies or external verifiers. Alan Smithers was certainly not alone in expressing concern about this area, and during 1994 and 1995 Government has put pressure on NCVQ and the awarding bodies to give more help to teachers, and has backed this up with some extra resources.

As we found in our local survey, these problems were often exacerbated because both teachers and students found the terminology in which the learning and assessment processes were expressed difficult to understand. The language of the official documentation was obscure and full of jargon, and some schools and colleges found it necessary to rewrite this in a simpler form for students. OFSTED, FEFC and the Department of Employment all criticised NCVQ for this, but FEFC believed that the situation was improving with time as schools and colleges became 'more comfortable with the new ways of describing courses' (FEFC, 1994b, p12). Similarly there was a broad consensus that too much staff and student time was spent on excessive paperwork and form filling. According to the FEFC Report, 'one college found that recording the progress of a single student required more than 400 separate written entries during a one year course' (FEFC, 1994b, p12). Despite the Government's commitment to change, teachers and students are continuing to say that, compared with teaching and learning, there is still too much emphasis on planning and recording.

GNVQs are basically articulated through their assessment frameworks and it is not surprising that much attention has been focused on assessment procedures and how these are setting standards. GNVQs have a complex, some would say 'unwieldy' assessment system which tends to reflect the different interests of those who set it up in the first instance. Although NCVQ did not apply its competence-based approach directly to GNVQs, the performance criteria are judged on a simple 'yes/no' basis. This is very much in line with Gilbert Jessup's ideological commitment to outcome assessment and also preserves a strong link with the approach used in NVQs. Again in line with Jessup's views, GNVQs do not permit a sampling approach to assessment, insisting that everything in a programme is tested and passed. Moreover, it is not possible to offset a poor performance in one area against a good one in another. The awarding bodies, and particularly BTEC, had considerable experience of institutions assessing their courses by assignments and projects, and there was considerable determination on their part to continue with this tradition as they believed it would preserve a broad educational dimension in the qualifications, not allowing them to be taken over by considerations of 'narrow training'. DES and higher education strongly supported this, but also insisted on GNVQs being subject to external testing to establish national standards. This was regarded as absolutely essential if parity with A levels was to be achieved.

Initially there was much criticism of the external multiple choice tests from tutors including several in our local survey. While some questions were remarkably simple, others seemed impossibly hard. Often the material was not trialled and there were problems with ambiguous questions. Colleges and schools were not supplied with specimen papers and at the outset did not know what to expect, but students were required to obtain the very high pass mark of 80 per cent (later reduced to 70 per cent). Although many of these teething problems were eventually solved, some issues proved much more intractable. Students are permitted to take the tests on several occasions, but they must pass if the GNVQ is to be awarded. However, the marks obtained in the tests do not affect the final grade given for the qualification. OFSTED is not convinced that multiple choice questions are capable of testing the more challenging aspects of the courses. Given their earlier stance, NCVQ and BTEC would probably be content to see the tests abolished altogether, but this is unlikely in the current situation when GNVQs are being established as a significant route into higher education.

OFSTED and FEFC also criticised aspects of the assessment of assignments. They reported too much variability in the thoroughness of assessment both within and between institutions with this being particularly pronounced at Intermediate level. More consistency in developing high quality and comparable assignments and in portfolio preparation were demanded. They stressed the need for more attention to be paid to the coordination of assessment across institutions, and OFSTED believed that assessment demands on teachers were still 'unduly time-consuming' and should be made more manageable.

Government reacted to these various criticisms of GNVQs from OFSTED, FEFC and commentators such as Alan Smithers. In March 1994, Tim Boswell, Minister of State for Education, announced an action plan to strengthen the rigour in GNVQs which included improving external testing, more training for external verifiers, clarifying the knowledge needed for a GNVQ and providing clearer guidance to teachers on marking coursework, grading and setting up and designing courses. These improvements were not made as swiftly as the inspectors wanted and expected, and by October, NCVQ was on the defensive about them. Boswell again confirmed that urgent action was in hand. Late in March 1995 NCVQ and the awarding bodies published a new guide to assessment entitled *GNVQ Quality Framework* which attempted to meet the earlier criticisms and set out new criteria for good practice in this area. Less than three months later it was announced that £21 million was being allocated to NCVQ, FEDA (Further Education Development Agency) and GEST (Grants for Education Support and Training) 'to secure rigour, quality and credibility for GNVQ' (*TES*, 9 June 1995). The Government's aim was 'to give a powerful kick-start to local and regional initiatives' (*TES*, 9 June 1995) in GNVQs, and there can be no doubt that there was a strong national commitment to make this enterprise successful.

Assessment and its refinement have almost become obsessions in GNVQ. Several studies have brought out the 'cumbersome and bureaucratic nature of NCVQ assessment', and Hyland argues that it is now time to abandon this 'in favour of something more like the GCSE and BTEC models of learning attainments and objectives' (Hyland, 1995). Although this would be controversial, the need for a better balance between learning and assessment is now broadly agreed. OFSTED, GARP (GNVQ Assessment Review Project) and Ron Dearing in his interim review of 16–19 education have all proposed that there should be exploration of how externally set and marked assignments can be incorporated into portfolio assessment at all three GNVQ levels. It is interesting that external GNVQ assessment has received so much attention and so often raised the temperature, when its predecessors such as BTEC First and National Diplomas were subjected to no external testing whatsoever and were handled altogether with a much lighter touch. This underlines the possibility that GNVQs are already being taken seriously as national qualifications comparable with GCSEs and A levels.

Grading of GNVQ has proved just as controversial as its assessment. NCVQ was unenthusiastic about its introduction in the first place, seeing it as inconsistent with its 'yes/no' competence approach to assessment. It was eventually conceded, however, that it was essential if parity with A levels was to be achieved. In their analyses of GNVQ both OFSTED and Smithers argued that performance in the external tests should contribute towards the award of merit and distinction grades. FEFC, OFSTED and tutors in our survey have all stressed how teachers and students are still unclear about how the criteria for the overall grading of GNVQ should be applied. Although NCVQ have issued several guidance booklets on the subject, evidence from OFSTED and our local sources suggests that practitioners are still far from clear and are adopting many different methods of determining final grades. This could easily undermine confidence in what distinctions and merits really represent and whether there is any consistency in the use of the terms between different institutions. This may become a cause of concern to higher education admissions tutors. Furthermore, compared with A levels, GNVQ grading remains a relatively blunt instrument. This has led to some discussion of whether a system of 'points scoring', already well established for A level entrants to universities, might be applied more widely across the 16–19 spectrum. Several influential professional bodies, particularly the headteachers' associations, are pursuing this issue with ministers expressing considerable interest. Developments on these lines could eventually transform, even supersede, the current GNVQ grading system.

There is some evidence that an important proportion of students admitted to Advanced GNVQ courses have lower entry requirements than those normally recommended by their institutions. The vast majority of young people with high GCSE grades continue to take A levels. Alison Wolf's research has shown that two-thirds of centres specify a minimum of four Cs at GCSE for entry to Advanced GNVQ, but, in practice, about half (49 per cent) of the students do not meet this criterion (FEU, Institute of Education and Nuffield Foundation, 1994, p31). She argues that Advanced GNVQ will have to continue to recruit significantly from this cohort if it is to meet the expansion targets planned for it by Government. On the other hand, John Hillier, chief executive of NCVQ, asserts that GNVQ is appealing to the whole ability range, but Wolf's more systematic investigation suggests that 'in the vast majority of cases Advanced GNVQs are being used as direct substitutes for BTEC Nationals and are attracting a comparable segment of the 16–19 population' (FEU, Institute of Education and Nuffield Foundation, 1994, p54) and they do not recruit many students who obtained outstanding GCSE results. The tendency to admit relatively low achieving students to GNVQ programmes has caused even more concern at Intermediate level. Many institutions operate a completely open admissions policy although others insist on certain requirements such as at least two Ds at GCSE. Wolf, like the teachers in our local survey, reported that students whose academic achievements were at the lower end of the scale found Intermediate GNVQ very difficult and FEFC believed that many inappropriately placed students left their courses early without an award. There was still considerable confusion amongst teachers about the level at which work for Intermediate should be pitched. These problems were noticed by OFSTED and FEFC in their inspections. Both bodies commented on the variations in standards in lessons and assignments. A disturbingly large proportion of work was unsatisfactory, and, according to OFSTED, this was particularly so in Leisure and Tourism and Manufacturing. Wolf's survey has shown that many Intermediate students want ultimately to progress to higher education, but their teachers question whether these are realistic aspirations. Our own investigation produced similar findings with many teachers doubting whether most of their current Intermediate students would be able to cope with Advanced GNVQ.

Despite certain problems, the introduction of GNVQs has received an overwhelmingly positive response from both students and their teachers. According to OFSTED (OFSTED, 1994), the chief sources of satisfaction are the degree of independence achieved by learners, the collaborative relationships, increased contact with business, commerce and community organisations and the breadth of scope the courses offered. In numerical terms Government has always been ambitious for GNVQs. In 1993 John Patten indicated that he wanted to see one quarter of all 16 year olds starting GNVQ courses by 1996. Early the following year Tim Boswell claimed that the equivalent of one in seven 16 year olds were now taking GNVQs, and in the longer term hoped that half of all 16 and 17 year olds would be on such courses. At times NCVQ expressed concern that expansion was happening too fast and feared schools would not be ready in time. Exaggerated claims were occasionally made in the press that thousands of 16 year olds were abandoning traditional A levels for the new vocational qualification, but Wolf's work has since shown clearly that this was not the case. Nonetheless, numerical expansion has been spectacular with over 162,000 students enrolled for GNVQs in 1994/95, only their second year of general availability. Of this total, 58,000 (35 per cent) were taking Business, 34,000 (21 per cent) Health and Social Care and 30,000 (18 per cent) Leisure and Tourism. About 1,000 (less than 1 per cent) were doing Manufacturing and just over 5,000 (3 per cent) Science. John Hillier of NCVQ and Sir Michael Lickiss of BTEC agree that the easy bit has been done so far and that soft targets such as full-time courses in business have been hit (*TES* 21 April 1995 and *Education,* 7 July 1995). They expect subjects such as Science and Manufacturing to continue to prove much more difficult as will recruiting part-time and older students. The achievements of GNVQ in these respects, however, should not be minimised, for it has already opened up an important route into higher education available via a nationally regulated vocational curriculum.

Considerable evidence has now been amassed showing that Advanced GNVQs are acceptable for entry to higher education courses. Almost all universities, except medical and dental schools, have agreed in principle to consider GNVQ students for degree and BTEC Higher National Diploma programmes. In 1994 and 1995 a very large proportion (between 85 per cent and 90 per cent) of applicants with Advanced GNVQs who applied for higher education received at least one offer. There is growing evidence that GNVQ applicants are largely orientated to vocational courses in new universities, often in their home localities. This trend may have been strengthened by new universities which have set up compacts with neighbouring colleges and schools and give priority to GNVQ students from the compact institutions. It may well be that there is less mutual interest and interaction between GNVQ students and the older, more traditional universities. More time is needed before a firm judgement can be made, but researchers such as Pat Ainley are already convinced that there are trends working towards 'mass higher education for the many combined with élite higher education for the few' (*TES*, 16 June 1995).

At the outset GNVQs were designed to provide a route either to higher education or to employment and further vocational training. Alan Smithers has always believed that the latter has been neglected, and has called for the purpose of GNVQs to be clarified. He is sceptical of the dual aims and argues that the training of technicians is not being well served by GNVQs. Early in 1994 NCVQ showed some concern about the higher education route becoming too dominant, and John Hillier claimed that, unlike A levels, GNVQs 'were primarily for entry into employment' (*THES*, 25 February 1994). BTEC has shown that 70 per cent of its GNVQ students are staying in full-time education and only 25 per cent going into jobs. This compares with 55 per cent of National Diploma students remaining in education and 39 per cent entering employment (*TES*, 7 July 1995). It has been shown beyond doubt that students see GNVQs primarily as an educational route providing progression to higher education, and Wolf urges Government and the universities to plan for this new influx of students, taking into account the level and type of their prior education achievements.

Such developments also have important consequences for colleges and schools. Several teachers in our survey stressed the likely emergence of the three year sixth form as some students followed Intermediate GNVQ with Advanced. Students have often been encouraged to take additional studies alongside their GNVQs. In further education there are financial reasons for doing this. In colleges a successfully completed Advanced GNVQ brings the funding for only two-thirds of a full-time student, and hence it is important to fill up students' timetables with other studies to supplement income. At present schools are funded differently and this factor does not apply. Consequently they may be willing to devote more hours to a GNVQ than colleges. Initially additional studies were normally justified in terms of facilitating entry to higher education. Students were often told that they needed to take a conventional A level alongside an Advanced GNVQ to have a realistic chance of obtaining an offer from a university, but increasing evidence is now casting doubt on this. Some students were encouraged to take additional GNVQ or NVQ units, but passing such qualifications does not seem to make any material difference to the outcome of university applications. Others take re-sit GCSEs, often trying to improve on grades below C obtained in English and mathematics. Rather surprisingly, by no means all GNVQ students with weaknesses in these two areas make the effort to re-sit and try to improve their grades. In the longer term it may become clearer how far GCSE performance is affecting chances of entry to higher education.

As GNVQs established themselves as a route into higher education and as they attempted to obtain high status including parity with A levels, most commentators (Hodkinson and Mattinson, 1994; Hyland, 1994; FEU, Institute of Education and Nuffield Foundation, 1994) argue that they have become more and more distant from their older cousins, NVQs. There is also a broad consensus that GNVQ has little chance of forming a bridge between 'the academic and vocational training tracks'. In Hodkinson's words, 'It is probable that the chasm between A levels and NVQs was always too wide to be bridged. In trying to bridge the unbridgeable, GNVQ has pulled towards the high status 'A' level side' (Hodkinson and Mattinson, 1994, p2). There is wide agreement that this will have undesirable consequences for students on the vocational training track who will become more isolated and provisions for them regarded as even lower in status. They will be 'on the periphery of the labour market' and 'left out in the cold' (Hyland, 1994, p113). It may have been such considerations which persuaded BTEC that it should not replace its National Diplomas in certain specialised vocational areas as quickly as originally envisaged. The further education lecturers working in these areas campaigned for and welcomed this decision, although NCVQ thought it unnecessary. There is now concern that GNVQs are not catering as well for those who will enter employment directly as for those who wish to go on to more advanced studies. It is possible that this pathway is in danger of being relatively neglected.

The massive expansion of GNVQs between 1992 and 1995 was unsurprising. Further education colleges were required in large measure to replace their older qualifications directly with GNVQs, and schools had been waiting for years for the arrival of a real alternative to A levels which enabled them to provide more appropriately for students who had performed in the middle or low/middle ranges at GCSE. In both sectors institutional funding was now structured to provide lucrative incentives to high student recruitment. In these circumstances it is difficult to see how GNVQs could have failed.

Because GNVQs developed first and foremost as an alternative route to higher education, the question of parity of esteem with the A level pathway remained a central concern. Ministers were equivocal on this subject. At times they implied that this was well on the way to being achieved, but on others it was stressed that Government could not grant this and it had to be earned. Schools and colleges have used GNVQs to provide for the needs of those students whose performance at GCSE was normally well below that of the higher fliers. Rarely have GNVQs recruited from that cohort of young people who have habitually followed A level courses. This can easily put GNVQ into a double bind. It is required to earn parity of esteem with A level, but must do so with a clientele which is, almost by definition, academically less strong. As the NEAB has said, 'It is a paradox that GNVQ has been introduced to meet the needs of students for whom 'A' level is considered inappropriate, and yet the two qualifications are intended to be of the same standard' (NEAB, 1995, p4). It would be fairer to put less emphasis on attaining parity of esteem and to acknowledge the essential differences which still exist. There is, however, lack of parity in another important area. NEAB has stressed that 'the two qualifications are designed and conducted by different bodies, are subject to different sets of rules and regulations and have different assessment regimes' (NEAB, 1995, p4). A level assessment still has a strong emphasis on conventional examinations and there is a severe, nationally imposed limit on the proportion of coursework. In contrast, it is often seen as virtuous that GNVQs are mainly assessed through coursework assignments with sparing use made of formal examinations. A level assessment assumes that candidates' abilities will be sampled, but such practices are not permitted in GNVQs. It is not easy to see a rationale for these discrepancies and the reasons why they need to be perpetuated.

With the merger between the Department for Education and the Department of Employment in the summer of 1995 and with the moves to bring together awarding bodies on opposite sides of the divide, it now seems possible that for the first time in this country the so-called 'academic' and 'vocational' curricula may be brought together under one framework. It is widely agreed amongst education and training professionals that such a development is long overdue.

CHAPTER 7

The Core Curriculum

One of the aims of the research upon which this book is based was to examine the whole curriculum in school sixth forms. While the last four chapters have focused on the different curriculum tracks and qualification components, the subject of this chapter is the unifying or core elements of the post-16 curriculum. Although the title of the chapter itself may be seen as conveying a greater certainty of the existence of a core curriculum than is perhaps justified by the evidence, the argument has been put many times, not least by the schools in our research, that the ideal of a core curriculum is worth striving for. However, before turning to a review of local and national attempts to bring the concept of a core curriculum to fruition, it is necessary to consider what is meant by a core curriculum and what purpose it might serve.

In pre-16 education the term 'core curriculum' is one that has been employed with a certain amount of consistency and maybe seen to equate with compulsory common elements in the curriculum. In the National Curriculum requirements for England and Wales the core curriculum is represented by the programmes of study of the various foundation subjects together with other compulsory elements such as Religious Education. Schools may of course seek to implement their own core curriculum that is wider than the statutory requirement. In the early years of education the extent of the planned statutory core curriculum is such that in practice it almost fills the whole of the formal curriculum. By Key Stage 4 pupils do, however, have greater freedom to choose from a range of subjects and academic and vocational qualifications. This flexibility of curriculum provision has increased since Sir Ron Dearing's review of the National Curriculum, but the fact remains that Key Stage 4 pupils in maintained schools must study certain elements including full courses in mathematics, English and at least a single science together with short courses in technology, a modern foreign language and physical education. Religious education, sex education and careers guidance are also compulsory.

The area covered by the core curriculum pre-16 is thus relatively fixed and common between maintained schools. However, in the non-compulsory post-16 education phase where the emphasis is on student choice within a greater diversity of routes, the concept of a core curriculum is more problematic.

In Chapter 4 we considered various attempts to broaden the post-16 academic curriculum in terms of optional or compulsory subject study. The debate, as a number of heads of sixth form commented, goes wider than the breadth of academic subjects and relates to a core entitlement of wider experiences and skills for all post-16 students. Writing with reference to the National Curriculum, Kelly has argued against an imposed knowledge-based curriculum but rather for a common curriculum that asserts:

> ...what every child is entitled to not in terms of subject knowledge but in terms of kinds of experience and intellectual and other forms of development, (leaving it) to the professionals to interpret this general prescription for each child in relation to the individual child's needs.

(Kelly, 1990, p120)

Though Kelly ducks his own argument relating to the difficulty of defining a 'need', the view expressed here is clearly translatable to the post-16 curriculum albeit with greater emphasis on guided self-determinism by the student. As one of head of sixth form explained, his wish was to see 'increased modularity in order to facilitate a greater individuality of a personal curriculum for students.' And yet balanced with this, even providing the external assertion of what all post-16 students must experience, is the view of the employers: 'As firms must anticipate change, they need employees with a breadth of ability. This means having core transferable skills such as communication, problem-solving and personal skills, which are essential in almost any business context' (CBI, 1993, p11).

Core skills

For employers, then, one of the keys to a successful business is seen to lie in having a skilful work force for whom important 'skills' are the abilities to transfer and adapt ways of working from one context to another and to learn new skills as business practices change. While individual occupations and higher education programmes may require certain bodies of knowledge and understanding, it is the so-called skills that are central both in terms of applying current knowledge and understanding and in responding to new situations. It is perhaps not surprising then that those arguing for a statutory post-16 curriculum entitlement, or less prosaically compulsion, should often express this desired common or core element of the curriculum in terms of communication (numeracy, literacy), the use of information technology, problem-solving and personal (individual and group) skills. It is the additional perception of 'core skills' as a potential unifying element across the different academic and vocational areas that makes them so appealing. The argument is that these are generic transferable skills that all young people should possess irrespective of their programme of study. It is, however, the very non-specificity of context that makes the definition, development, assessment and accreditation of core skills so problematic.

Furthermore the term 'core skill' is not limited to those mentioned above but is used liberally in post-16 education to denote a wide range of curricular components that can only loosely be defined as skills. Different participants in the core skills debate have at various times included forms of communication, modes of working, attitudes, understanding and cross-curricular themes. A helpful review of the different uses and terms used is provided by the FEU in *Core Skills in Action* (FEU, 1992). Leaving aside the definitions and nomenclature, the unifying aspect though is that these 'core skills' are deemed to be of central importance to all young people and are focused less on subject knowledge but more on the ability to achieve a particular goal in a range of familiar and unfamiliar contexts.

As has been seen in Chapter 1 the movement for the inclusion of core skills in the post-16 curriculum goes back further than the debates and policy proposals initiated in 1989 by Kenneth Baker. However, it was the then Secretary of State's speech to the Association for Colleges of Further and Higher Education early that year that can be seen to have prefigured much of the current debate on proposals for including core skills in all post-16 programmes.

Building on the thinking and developmental work of the MSC and other non-governmental agencies such as BTEC, Baker laid down his view of core skills as both a broadening and a unifying device in post-16 education. This view of core skills was subsequently developed by HMI in *Post-16 Education and Training, Core skills: an HMI paper* (DES, 1989) with other organisations including the CBI and TUC contributing important policy statements on core skills. The agreement on the need for some sort of 'core skills' seemed to be growing though what should be counted as core skills and how these should relate to a student's programme of study was still far from resolved.

Responding to the subsequent request from the following Secretary of State, John MacGregor, for advice on the place of core skills in the post-16 curriculum, the NCC proposed a list of six groups of core skills. The NCC had focused on the academic curriculum as requested and classed the skills in two main categories. The first category comprised the groups of core skills which could form part of and be assessed in all curriculum areas (communication skills, problem-solving skills and personal skills) and the second those skills which it would not be appropriate nor possible to include in all A and AS syllabuses (numeracy, information technology and modern language competence) and which would need to be individually mapped and possibly supplemented in a compensatory way according to an individual's programme of study. Within this second category the NCC distinguished the first two skills which could be attached to and form part of a number of syllabuses from the third one of modern language competence which would need special provision outside of most A level syllabuses.

In the first category of skills which could form part of all syllabuses, the NCC proposed that the assessment of core skills should affect a student's A level grade – arguing that 'Core skills and subject knowledge and understanding are inseparable, but their relative contribution to a final grade should be formalised and made explicit' (NCC, 1990, p17).

NCC concluded its response by stating that the 'development of a common framework for core skills across all post-16 qualifications will assist progression and transfer' (ibid., p23) and by recommending a programme of further work on core skills, both pre- and post-16. A parallel response from NCVQ followed, confirming a large measure of agreement on the proposed core skills and underlining the potential for linking the academic and vocational post-16 sectors. SEAC also broadly supported the movement towards the assessment of core skills as part of academic qualifications, and following the acceptance by the DES of the NCC list of core skills, included the integration of core skills in A and AS level syllabuses in its draft A and AS principles. However, it soon became apparent that the Prime Minister, Margaret Thatcher, was not prepared to see any substantial change to A levels. SEAC's position on the integration of core skills in post-16 academic qualifications was subsequently revised and in the final version of the A and AS principles the compulsory inclusion of core skills in syllabuses was no longer being proposed.

Though work on core skills in academic qualifications continued in 1991, with SEAC exemplifying the role and assessment of core skills in A and AS level, it began to assume a declining priority. Lawson has highlighted a major constraint imposed on the development of core skills by John MacGregor who warned 'it is essential that nothing be done to prejudice the A level standards based upon academic rigour and study in depth. If core skills can be embedded in syllabuses without prejudicing those standards well and good' (reported in Lawson, 1992, p90). SEAC finally concluded that core skills could not be included in A level assessment, lending themselves more to a record of achievement.

The development of core skills in the NVQ system, on the other hand, was taken forward with renewed impetus during 1991 and 1992 as the government reaffirmed support for national vocational provision by adding the new qualification of GNVQs to the NVQ framework. Working from the list of core skills put forward by the NCC and developed by NCVQ and SEAC, work was undertaken to establish a series of core skills units within the vocational framework. As the development and trialling of the draft core skills units by NCVQ and the vocational lead bodies progressed, adjustments were made to the titles and definitions of the core skill areas and the number of levels was increased from the original four to five so as to link with the five levels of the NVQ vocational areas. In line with NCC thinking, units in the different areas of modern languages competence were devised separately from the other core skills. A detailed report of this stage of the development of the core skills units is given by Oates (Oates, 1992) who reports that because of government concern about the consistency of assessment of personal skills and problem-solving skills the focus was placed on communication skills and application of number/numeracy (together with information technology) forming as they did a requirement of the proposed Advanced Diploma. This shift of emphasis was therefore in line with governmental concern to increase achievement in the basic skills of literacy and numeracy and the use of IT and matched more closely the core subjects of the National Curriculum. Nevertheless, while employers have indeed expressed concern about standards in these basic skills they have also emphasised the importance of flexible employees who can adapt and improve their own performance, work in teams and solve problems, a cause which was not assisted by the lower priority accorded to the personal (individual and team) skills and the problem-solving skills.

NCVQ's original intention and expectation that the core skills units should become a mandatory component of NVQs has yet to be achieved, with doubt expressed over the extent to which the generic core skills can be said to be equally applicable, demonstrable and assessable in the differing vocationally-specific areas. There is also a concern not to disenfranchise any competent and skilled employees who might not be able to achieve the required level in a particular core skill, though this statement in itself contained a certain irony. However, while the core skills units have not yet become a compulsory element of the NVQs, they have occupied a central role in GNVQs from their introduction in September 1992. The current position may be summarised as follows:

> The core skills units in 'Application of Number', 'Communication' and 'Information Technology' are compulsory at the appropriate level in all GNVQ areas and are available at five levels as are the core skills units in 'Improving own Learning and Performance' and 'Working with Others'. These latter units are not compulsory but may be taken as additional GNVQ units as can the NVQ modern languages units developed by the Languages Lead Body. The opportunity is also open to approved centres to offer any of the above core skills units as free-standing units to students taking other academic or vocational qualifications.

From the outset, NCVQ made it clear that it wished to see the core skills units integrated into the teaching of the vocational programmes rather than being taught in isolation as discrete skills. The NCVQ core skills development team used the following as a description of how it saw integration in practice:

> Successful integration of core skills units: occurs where the core skills are acquired through settings which contextualise the core skills in ways meaningful to students. Students should not see the core skills as something abstract and isolated. They should understand how the skills might be applied in future settings.
>
> (Oates and Harkin, 1995, p187)

However, in its first report on GNVQs, OFSTED found that: 'In many schools core skills requirements were considered late in the course and in several cases were not covered effectively' (OFSTED, 1992, para. 50). OFSTED concluded that: 'Overall, the planning and implementation of core skills requires more attention and schools need better guidance on these aspects from awarding bodies' (ibid.). In its second report, published in 1994, whilst pleased with improvements in some areas, OFSTED found that: 'the overall picture of core skills not being applied in their vocational context was disappointing' (OFSTED, 1994, para. 38). They also found that:

The standards of work in lessons designed to cover the **core skills** units in isolation from the vocational units (application of number, communication and IT) at all levels were barely satisfactory. There were few examples of good work stemming from the range requirements of the core skills units. (Original emphasis)

(ibid., para. 32)

The Further Education Funding Council in its report in November 1994 also commented on the failure of some teachers to 'recognise the importance of developing and assessing core skills through vocational work' (FEFC, 1994b, p5). However, the FEFC inspectors seek to identify the reasons for this shortcoming, suggesting that: 'Overall, the organisation and support for core skills are lagging behind those given to mandatory and optional units and their development is proving difficult to cover fully within these units' (ibid., p21).

Thus whilst HMI and FEFC concurred with NCVQ in asserting that the most effective way of developing core skills is by integrating them into the vocational context, not all schools and colleges are able or willing to provide the necessary staff training and resources to enable such core skills development to take place. Nonetheless, the increasing importance placed on core skills, as reflected in their mandatory status in GNVQ and in their acceptance by many organisations as a potentially significant part of the academic curriculum, does place the onus on institutions to make clear provision for core skills in their post-16 curriculum.

Core activity programmes

Nearly all the sixth forms that we surveyed were able to outline some form of core curriculum though, as we noted in Chapter 2, there was great variation in both the extent and form this took. In a small number of schools core skills took a central position in the core provision in an attempt to unify the academic and vocational elements of the sixth form curriculum. For many others though the 'core curriculum' differed according to whether the vocational or the academic track was being followed by students. For instance, in the former case all students might be expected to undertake a core skills GNVQ programme while in the latter a general or minority studies programme might be provided with little or no reference to core skills. It is to this latter more traditional form of provision that we shall turn first.

In these general or minority studies programmes the focus was very often provided by A or AS level General Studies, though whether or not GCE A level students would automatically be entered for the General Studies examination (and at which level) was usually dependent on performance in mock examinations. In the event many students are entered and this is testified to by the continuing buoyancy of the A level General Studies entry figures with over 57,000 candidates in Summer 1995. The entry level thus remains high despite criticisms that the A level General Studies examination is an outdated attempt to bridge the arts/science divide and broaden the individual's narrow academic school curriculum, when the focus should be on building breadth into the whole curriculum and providing a coherent programme. Smithers and Robinson have criticised General Studies for being 'a particular approach to breadth, treating it as a separate examinable subject' (Smithers and Robinson, 1993, p25) and have seen in its continued existence a risk that a full and rational debate on breadth will not take place while this apparently neat solution remains. Likewise they perceive a danger in revising or abolishing the General Studies examination without a careful consideration of the purpose and form of a broad curriculum.

While giving General Studies a central place in their core provision, heads of sixth form in the schools in our research appeared uncertain about whether this was the best means of promoting breadth. Varying approaches had been taken including programmes of visiting speakers, sessions by teachers from different areas of the curriculum, discussion formats and even coaching in examination technique though few expressed satisfaction with their provision.

Students reported almost unanimously that General Studies lessons were not taken seriously by themselves nor often, they suspected, by their teachers. The General Studies A level examination was seen by students as something that had to be done which might help with entry to Higher Education. Indeed one head of sixth form admitted that this was the reason students were encouraged to take the examination:

A lot of students these days seem to be getting in more and more with a General Studies point and it seems as though the trend is that General Studies is becoming more and more acceptable. So particularly for the students doing two A levels we think it's probably better if we try and build it up a little bit.

Other teachers saw inherent value in the content of the General Studies syllabuses. One commented: 'I teach General Studies and am more and more appalled at how little they know. The students are very, very conservative', and another that 'General Studies is really important because that's one of the few subjects where they do have to keep a broad perspective, they find that difficult at times.' Interestingly, of the two independent schools in our research project one did not offer General Studies and the other was considering abandoning it. In both cases this was to free up time for students either to improve their A level grades or to take on another minority subject or a fourth A level.

The ambiguity in schools towards General Studies seems to arise from the fact that heads of sixth form are seeking accreditation for a programme whose aim is to give students a wider experience and perspective from an examination whose purpose is to test a range of subject understanding and general knowledge. This mismatch between the provision and the means of accreditation was highlighted by one head of sixth form:

> We have General Studies for two year students, a sort of mish-mash, partly aimed at trying to prepare them for AS or A level exam but also...well we fall between two stools really with General Studies, obviously we want to do as much as we can to help students pass the exam, but also to further things that all sixth form students should have experience of before they leave.

The relationship between the examination and the provision is often uncertain and at times not intended. A number of schools have simply decided what experiences their students would benefit from and provided these in a coherent programme, putting the students in for the General Studies examination almost as an optional extra. At least in these schools there was a clearer focus on the aims of the minority programme and the sort of breadth that was sought.

Some schools were seeking to unify the academic and vocational curriculum tracks through the provision of a common minority studies programme. Nevertheless, even where a core studies programme was compulsory across the sixth form, the wide range of provision, coupled with optional elements, meant that in essence a core curriculum as such did not exist in many cases. Between schools there was little evidence of even general agreement on the purpose and forms of such a programme, and the variation due to individual staff availability, interests and philosophies was high. The following examples and comments on core studies programmes content will serve to give a flavour of the range and types of provision on offer:

> Optional Activities – available for all students by request – sports and leisure activities, information technology and work experience.

> Enrichments programme – students choose three courses per year from the following: first aid, photography, cookery, archaeology,

Amnesty International/human rights issues, interior design, physical education, information technology, outdoor pursuits.

Short courses for all A level students: Problem solving/Mathematical Thinking, Shakespeare's plays, Information Technology, Politics, Moral Awareness, Modern Language Competence.

All sixth formers have careers, Recreational Activities and a tutorial programme, additionally those in Year 12 take part in the DVE programme unless they are taking a four A level course. Year 13 do General Studies. All Year 12 have two weeks' work experience at the end of the Summer term – many to France and Germany.

We have PSE for 25 minutes every morning, one period per week tutor period. A whole variety of things are done, some compulsory, some optional, e.g. vocational students might be doing work on core skills, A level students doing something on applying to HE, people just about to leave working on CVs. We have things like health education for everyone, 'Skills for Living', at the moment we're in the middle of a Student Masterchef competition where groups have to produce a meal for £2.50, money management, all those sorts of skills.

Quite a wide core, I'm fairly proud of it. I would hate to see it go, but it is at risk. We have a ten day 50 period timetable and a core of nine periods – it consists of three General Studies periods, one of which is a plenary session with films or visiting speakers, the other two are taught on a rotation system, languages, science, maths, etc. The vast majority take General Studies as an A level. Two periods on basic PE or fitness. We give a range of opportunities, but it is compulsory. Four periods of recreational activities (voluntary work, outdoor pursuits, first aid, cookery, painting, etc). It's been introduced over the last 7 or 8 years. I'd be loath to see it go although conscious that other schools don't offer anything on that scale. It's costing enormously in staffing terms...OFSTED highlighted outstanding extra curricular activities – outdoor activities, music, drama, trips, very good social life – coach trips, etc. The totality of the sixth form experience is much more than formal curriculum we've been talking about.

As will be clear from this last example, the financial cost of providing an extensive compulsory programme, beyond a common tutorial programme, is not insignificant and this point was made by a number of schools concerned about the funding of this marginalised area. Another serious constraint in providing a programme common to all sixth formers was that of timetabling.

While some schools presented students with pre-specified option blocks for A level subjects, the general pattern was for schools to take account of provisional subject choices and patterns in drawing up the A level timetable blocks. The desire for flexibility to meet the increasingly diverse patterns of subject choice and co-timetabling with GNVQ A levels to allow mixing of routes had led to some schools using nearly all the available timetable space for subject blocks. This had restrictive implications for common time across the sixth form in which to offer other certificated courses such as AS levels and core or minority studies:

> We don't give option blocks. We collect information on what they want and do try and arrange the timetable – next year only two haven't got what they wanted. This is at the expense of time left over for everyone to do PE together or Work Experience or Community Service. All 40 periods per week are taken up by subjects.

While core skills provision in GNVQ was necessarily more developed than elsewhere in the curriculum, with some schools putting on hour workshops for each core skill, only a small minority of schools had implemented a programme focusing on core skills that was common to all GCE and GNVQ A level students. One example was to be found in a sixth form with comparable numbers of students on academic and vocational courses. Here all GCE and GNVQ A level students have to follow a common core skills programme based on GNVQ core skills – communication, information technology, numeracy and problem-solving. There is also a tutorial programme, with sports activities, work experience, residential activities and community programmes optional. The head of sixth form commented:

> Greatest satisfaction from this job is knowing that by end of Year 12 every student is IT competent, all coursework for A level word processed, all personal statements for UCAS on disk. They do more than word processing, also data processing, it's a vital competence nowadays.

This clear focus on core skills within a common programme bridging the academic–vocational divide was sadly lacking in many sixth forms though two schools had plans to introduce such a programme the following year. A small group of schools saw it as a longer-term development and one school was intending to introduce a modern foreign language for all sixth-formers. The general lack of such core programmes notwithstanding, many heads of sixth form and GNVQ coordinators were in favour of a more coherent provision and one TVEI coordinator commented:

> I regret the demise of the Wessex project and the stop put on

exploratory work on modularising A levels and interchange with GNVQ. I hope that momentum does survive. I would like to see students initially choosing one particular route but being able to move across, to take credit for the things they have done. There's a place for academic and vocational routes with equal status but there must be flexibility to interchange. A level might have mix of academic and vocational or all academic or all vocational. Don't see necessarily any problem with that other than people's attitudes.

One school had seen possibilities for linking the academic and vocational routes within the current framework using DVE and then GNVQ modules as options for GCE A level students but had met resistance from these students, and their parents, who had not seen the value in Higher Education entry terms of the additional free-standing units and had consequently not opted for them in significant numbers:

> On the Health and Social Care one we've got a foundation course for counselling skills. Well if you're going into medicine, for example, we always have a couple who are every year, or into nursing, and we certainly have some of those, or you're interested in Psychology courses, anything of that kind, then really they ought to be picking that unit up, but they're not. It's one of 'Oh I've got too much work on'....I don't think, not in my experience anyway, that we're going to have massive success if we carry on simply giving people talks, you know, little pep talks in assembly telling them how much this stuff would enhance their curriculum if only they took it.

Another sixth form had a greater amount of success with mixing GCE and GNVQ subjects within the current framework:

> I think there's more potential with GNVQ (than with BTEC) and more potential for the school to mix provision across the sixth form, e.g. mixed groups of A and GNVQ business students. We have about six students doing Advanced Business (following a mixed course): two or three doing A level French; one or two doing AS Technology; someone doing Business and A level Computer Studies. We set up the timetable to leave one A level block free for students in GNVQ Advanced to choose from. It includes AS Maths, A level History, French. We're going to offer some additional units in MFL, that's the next move forward, bringing in additional units which GNVQ and A level students will have the opportunity to study.

In general, though, schools were looking to a national framework to provide coherence between both the 14–16 and the 16–19 phases of education and the academic and vocational tracks. For some this was at the level of holding the two routes together with bridges and ladders.

Others wished to see a unified curriculum integrating the academic and vocational aspects, perhaps through a modular credit accumulation scheme. This, it was felt would not only be less divisive, but allow greater coherence and flexibility at the same time and open-up the option of co-teaching GNVQ and GCE A levels. It was recognised nonetheless that the latter situation would involve an overhaul of the assessment system and the teaching and learning styles used in some A level classes. One head of sixth form observed, 'it would be good for some students, but for the majority it would be a culture shock to go into an A level subject, be like working for two bosses, two completely different ways of operating.' The difficulties anticipated would not only be at the student level but would relate to comparability and the understanding of what achievement of the different modules would mean. Stanton's analogy with different maps for the academic, GNVQ and NVQ pathways is pertinent here:

> The maps use different scales, and each has its own benchmarks against which to measure the length of the journey and level reached. None of the routes has a measurement for breadth. Even the conventions used in order to describe standard features (such as core content) vary.
>
> (Stanton, 1994, p251)

Despite the problems that might be raised there was a general consensus that there was a need to address the disparity of esteem between academic and vocational qualifications. Some respondents were in favour of compulsory vocational units for all sixth form students, others saw the introduction of core skills into GCE A syllabuses and common teaching as a possible solution. One questionnaire respondent argued that one way to give currency to Advanced GNVQ would be to have modular A courses with core modules that can form part of GNVQ courses.

16–19 Review

Standing back from the demands for further 16–19 developments and initiatives, three questionnaire respondents made a plea for some stability until the current system had bedded down and two interviewees asked that a thought be spared for the timetabler if an intricate cross-qualification system were to be implemented in sixth forms. However, despite reassurances about a five year moratorium on development in the pre-16 curriculum, the government subsequently announced that Sir Ron Dearing had been asked to review post-16 curricular provision and coherence so as to advise the government on 'ways to strengthen, consolidate and improve the framework of 16–19 qualifications' (Dearing, 1995, para. 1.1).

The terms of the Dearing 16–19 review were limited by the explicit request to work with the existing qualifications of A levels, GNVQs and NVQs. Accepting the remit given, the issues addressed by Dearing in the second stage of the review centred on how best to relate the differing pathways in a coherent framework so that there 'need be no barrier to students combining vocational and academic studies or to students earning credits in one pathway which can be transferred to a related programme in another pathway' (Dearing, 1995, para. 6.2).

The form that a new credit framework encompassing the three pathways might take has been the subject of much work by the FEU who have been promoting the need for a clear and coherent framework post-16 and, more recently post-14, for a number of years (see FEU, 1995 for a summary). The direction of Dearing's 16–19 review was also clearly influenced by the joint statement by six of the headteachers and college principals' associations in October 1994 which, as we have seen, argued for a coherent and flexible framework to permit credit transfer.

With regard to the further development of core skills post-16 Dearing sought to respond to a question posed by the Secretary of State: 'And should we encourage core skills, which are already an essential part of GNVQs, as part of the programmes of study for more 16 to 19 year olds? I believe we should.' (*DfE News* 79/95.) The permission to proceed again along the route of core skills in post-16 academic qualifications was clearly signalled, though Dearing may have gone further than was intended in considering core skills other than those which are compulsory in GNVQs. The case for these three core skills had been strengthened by their inclusion in the new National Targets for Education and Training announced in the revised White Paper *Competitiveness: forging ahead* (DTI, 1995) where the relevant targets were for 75 per cent of 19 year olds to achieve Level 2 and 35 per cent of 21 year olds to achieve Level 3 by the year 2000. Given the short timescale set, the need for post-16 core skills action is self-evident. Following the initial consultation phase of the 16–19 review, Dearing reports that the National Advisory Council for Education and Training Targets was itself in favour of the incorporation of the GNVQ core skills units of 'Improving own Learning and Performance' and 'Working with Others' in all programmes of study and that the CBI had a similar position (cf. CBI, 1993, pp17–18) and foresaw the need for modern language competence to be a specified core skill (Dearing, 1995, p28).

Dearing's concerns in the 16–19 review were not only to decide the extent to which the different core skills should form part of all post-16 programmes of study but how the development of these skills should be planned, assessed and accredited; a key question for the 16–19 review being whether or not the core skills could be taught and assessed through the different A and AS level syllabuses. Pring has pointed to 'logical problems in defining these 'skills' generically, i.e. in abstraction from the particular contexts and subject areas where they are applied' (Pring, 1994, p5), though much effort has been put into addressing this potential problem in the case of GNVQs where core skills are delivered and assessed through the vocational areas being studied, often with workshop support. On the other hand the consideration of an advanced national certificate to record achievement in core skills separately from GCE and GNVQ subject areas parallels in many ways the proposal of an Advanced Diploma mooted and then abandoned by John Major.

Before concluding this chapter it is worth considering the alternative but complementary model for a core curriculum provided by the skills-based Diploma of Achievement. This post-16 course available from the Oxford and Cambridge Schools Examination Board (OCSEB) aims to encourage 'self-reliance, flexibility and breadth' (OCSEB, 1994, p3) by developing competence and recording achievement in a range of core skills (Designing and Making, Computing, Surviving, Numeracy, Organising, Investigating, Communicating) through a selection of themes (e.g. Family Issues, Industry, Towards a Personal Philosophy, European Dimension, Ethical Issues, Health). The Diploma thus seeks to provide the core content of cross-curricular themes relevant to young people and to use these as the context for developing core skills and understanding. The course may therefore provide support for the development of core skills within a GCE or GNVQ programme of study or as the principal means of core skill development. It will be interesting to follow the take-up and implementation of this Diploma course introduced in September 1995, to see whether it can serve as a vehicle for the raising of standards of achievement in core skills with the additional prospect of providing a basis for the development of a broader core curriculum of knowledge, understanding and attitudes.

Whatever approach to the implementation of core skills schools and colleges take in the wake of Dearing's proposals, they will need to consider how best to plan for the development of the individual core skills to ensure that they are not overlooked nor accorded a second-rate priority by students or teachers and tutors. Structures will also need to be put in place to map, assess and accredit work taking place elsewhere in the student's personal curriculum so as to avoid duplication. This of course equally applies to pre-16 work and raises the issue of consistency of assessment in differing contexts.

As we have seen above from the schools in the research project, the development of core skills does not in itself necessarily imply a common or core curriculum. It is perfectly possible for the academic and vocational tracks to have similar but separate core skills provision. Indeed with core skills embedded in GNVQ programmes this situation can easily come about. Furthermore core skills are in themselves only one element of a core curriculum which must seek to give post-16 students access to wider curricular breadth of content and understanding as illustrated by the Diploma of Achievement. The challenge facing schools and colleges is to build on Dearing's proposals for core skills, credit transfer and common certification in such a way that academic and vocational pathways are not merely coexisting in the same structural system but share the common provision of a broad core curriculum.

CHAPTER 8

Guidance and Information for Prospective Post-16 Students

One of the aims of the Conservative government in the field of social policy has been to introduce a quasi-market system into public services which remain largely taxpayer funded and free at the point of delivery. The optimal operation of the market is premised upon the actions of individuals making rational choices from a range of alternatives. In this way virtue will be rewarded and those who are less virtuous will be encouraged to improve. More specifically, in the field of education, schools and colleges which are providing the services which their customers want will flourish, while those which are not will either go to the wall or improve their offerings to the point where they can compete in the market place. Within this social and economic theory the provision of information is vitally important. The optimisation of the system depends upon the actions of thousands of well-informed and hence rationally-acting consumers. In the absence of comprehensive and accurate information there is a danger that the virtuous will be unrewarded while those lacking virtue will flourish. (Of course, most advocates of the market would acknowledge that it rarely works in the pure, untrammelled way suggested by the theory, but would argue that even if there are distortions and imperfections in its operation it remains a better method of allocating resources than any of the alternatives). In the context of an increasingly market-driven education system the provision of information and guidance to young people on the options available to them post-16 takes on considerable importance.

It is not necessary to accept fully the ideology of choice and individualism which is at the heart of much current government policy on education and training to acknowledge that there are elements of choice available to 16 year olds as they end their period of compulsory education. There are essentially three dimensions of choice: (i) whether to stay-on in full-time education or leave school and obtain a full-time job or enter YT; (ii) for those staying-on in full-time education, which course of study to choose; (iii) for those staying-on in full-time education, which institution to attend. Of course for many individuals these choices will be severely constrained. For example, in many areas of the country and in some occupational sectors full-time employment for 16 year-olds has virtually disappeared. For many youngsters their GCSE results also restrict their opportunities to enter courses of study – a 16 year old who does not obtain any GCSEs at grades A–C effectively has little or no chance of entering a GCE A level programme. For many 16 year olds, particularly those living in rural areas, practical difficulties of transport and finance may severely limit their choice of institutions. Family and social class circumstances may also constrain choices. For students from poor families it may be difficult to forgo the YT allowance and obtain the financial support necessary to stay on in full-time education. For others, selection of courses of study may be constrained by cultural attitudes. For example, students from middle-class families where one or both parents are graduates might well be discouraged from entering vocational courses. In short, it is important not to be seduced by the ideology of the market into believing that structural and cultural constraints on student choices at 16 have somehow disappeared or become unimportant. On the other hand it is also illegitimate to assume that there is no element of personal choice available to 16 year olds and that everything is determined by an individual's position within the nexus of class, race, gender and geography.

Thus in what follows we assume that there are degrees of choice available to 16 year olds while acknowledging that these choices will be constrained in varying degrees by a range of social and economic circumstances. In this chapter we will use our data to examine the provision of information to students in Year 11 in the schools on the options available to them post-16. This is an issue which has been given considerable attention by policy-makers in recent times. For example the White Paper *Competitiveness: forging ahead* (DTI, 1995) argued for the provision of effective and impartial guidance on the options available post-16. The White Paper proposed that the OFSTED Framework of Inspection should be amended so that inspectors would seek evidence on the provision of good careers education and impartial guidance.

There are two related issues which arise from the provision of information and advice to students on their options post-16. The first relates to the extent to which the information is neutral and unbiased. Here there is clearly potential conflict between the provision of such information and the competition between institutions for post-16 students. This is likely to be particularly acute in schools with sixth forms. It is obviously in the interests of the schools to maximise the numbers of students who stay-on in their sixth forms and there is a temptation for schools to limit or distort the information which is given to students about other post-16 providers. We gave a flavour in Chapter 1 of the passions which this issue arouses. Colleges have been concerned that schools have not been passing on full information about college courses. Taylor (Taylor, 1992) in her study of ten Surrey schools found that there were wide variations between schools in the amount of information which they provided on post-16 options and that 12–18 schools did little to publicise college courses. HMI in their 1990 survey of guidance in schools identified as one of the shortcomings: 'the glossing over in some schools with sixth forms of further education or other educational alternatives at 16+'. They recognised the pressures on schools but were trenchant in their criticism:

> Of particular concern among the various shortcomings was the failure in some schools with sixth forms to present fully to students the various alternatives to staying on in the sixth form. This was due in part to the well-established concern of schools to retain good students so as to provide the basis for a sixth form of quality. It was reinforced by the desire to have a large sixth form, so as to be able to benefit from the financial benefits available under the Local Management of Schools if students are retained. While it is easy to understand the schools' point of view, it is difficult to see how they can justify putting their own interests before those of students.
>
> (HMI, 1990, p6)

Our evidence suggests that little has changed in the intervening years. The state of affairs referred to by HMI and Taylor was thoroughly predictable, as one of our teacher informants put it: 'You wouldn't expect Tesco's to advertise Sainsbury's would you?' Clearly not, but whereas in choosing between supermarkets it is possible to try Tesco's one week and Sainsbury's the next, this is hardly possible in the provision of post-16 education and training. In this context one 'supermarket' has had day-to-day access to the customer for several years in ways which are denied to competitors. We will show that in some schools there was pressure on 16 year olds to stay on at the school where they took their GCSEs. This, and the absence of fair and adequate information on the alternatives, threatens the operation of the market and hence the systemic improvements which its proponents claim will flow from its operation.

A second issue in relation to the provision of information and advice on post-16 options concerns the high non-completion and non-success rates from post-16 courses. This was strongly highlighted by the Audit Commission report (Audit Commission/OFSTED, 1993). The Commission stated that: 'Typically, between 30 per cent and 40 per cent of students enrolling on a course do not succeed, and for many courses the proportion is much higher' (p1). Non-completion rates were 13 per cent for A level courses and 18 per cent for vocational courses although on some courses non-completion rates were as high as 80 per cent. Non-completion was described as a 'source of significant waste in 16–19 education' (Audit Commission/OFSTED, 1993, p2). The Commission argued that: 'It would be impractical to eradicate failure and non-completion, but losses on this scale justify increased efforts to persuade more students to complete their courses and to match students and courses more appropriately' (p2).

Clearly for the Commission part of the solution to the problem of non-completion and non-success in full-time post-16 courses lay in better advice and guidance to students. Again, however, it is apparent that there is a possible contradiction between advising students on the most appropriate courses and the imperatives on schools and colleges to recruit as many post-16 students as possible. At present institutions are funded mainly on the basis of enrolment rather than completion or success in courses and while it would be going beyond the evidence to suggest that institutions recruit students irrespective of their chances of completion or success there clearly are strong pressures encouraging recruitment of borderline cases.

In the sections which follow we review our evidence on these issues. Before we do this it is important to bear in mind the limitations of this evidence. These arose principally from our research emphasis on curriculum policy and provision. Investigation of the information and guidance on post-16 options was somewhat peripheral to the main focus of our research. Our data was obtained through the questionnaires sent to schools with sixth forms and interviews with sixth formers, Year 11 students and appropriate staff conducted during our school visits. We did not visit or survey 11–16 schools or colleges.

While our focus on 11–18 schools has the advantage of illuminating the institutional context within which there are the greatest problems in terms of the provision of unbiased advice, it must be remembered that it ignores 11–16 schools where other research suggests advice on post-16 options is more satisfactory. Also, by definition, we spoke only to sixth formers who had chosen to stay on at school (almost all at the same school) rather than those who left to go to college or enrolled in a training scheme. Thus what follows is a partial rather than comprehensive examination of the issue of the choice of post-16 options. Despite these limitations we believe our data illuminates some important issues related to this currently controversial topic.

An overview of the post-16 options guidance curriculum

Before considering the three dimensions of choice open to students at post-16 we describe briefly the programme of guidance on post-16 options offered in the schools. Our questionnaire data revealed that there were five elements to post-16 options guidance which were offered in Year 11 in virtually all the schools. These were:

- a structured teaching input during a Personal and Social Education/ Careers course
- individual interviews with school staff
- parents evenings
- sixth form prospectus
- individual interviews with careers service staff.

In addition to these five elements about 75 per cent of the schools held a careers convention for Year 11 students. A variety of other sources of information were offered by a smaller number of schools. These included taster courses after GCSE examinations, talks from sixth formers, visits to colleges and training providers, visits from students at 11–16 schools, sixth form open days or evenings.

It appears from our data that most schools had a relatively comprehensive programme and when we asked what changes schools would like to see in their guidance procedures only about half of our respondents replied and of those who did the most common response was that they were 'Happy with it' or did not wish to see any changes. Among those who did wish to see changes the most common themes were to have greater time for guidance, to be able to start the process earlier (possibly in Year 9 or 10) and to have greater involvement of subject teachers. A small number of schools wanted greater parental involvement. The clear overall conclusion from our data, however, is that contrary to the criticisms which have been made of guidance by colleges, the Audit Commission and HMI changes in the procedures are not high among the priorities of the schools in our survey. Interestingly, despite the calls made by the Audit Commission for the use of value-added data at A level, only one of the schools responding to the questionnaire showed any interest in developing systematic use of the predictive power of GCSE results when guiding students on post-16 options.

However, when considering the adequacy of the guidance curriculum it is important to place it in context. As noted above the main structured input is during PSE/Careers courses. There is evidence that time for this work has been squeezed by the demands of the National Curriculum. A survey conducted for the Institute of Careers Guidance and the National Association of Careers and Guidance Teachers in 1992 concluded that:

> There is evidence to suggest that careers education is being squeezed out of the curriculum by the core and foundation subjects. It is also clear that many schools are having some difficulty in establishing cross-curricular careers education and finding time for discrete careers education in Key Stage 4.
>
> (Cleaton, 1993, p88)

Our own recent evaluation of Year 11 careers education and guidance in Rochdale LEA found similar concerns (Williams, Higham and Yeomans, 1994). In Rochdale there were also familiar anxieties about the consistency of the delivery of careers education in Year 11 within schools. PSE/Careers courses are often taught by non-specialist staff who have time available on their timetables after fulfilling their mainstream teaching commitments. This is symptomatic of the generally low status of careers and PSE work in schools. In these circumstances quality often varies considerably. It is probably significant that our questionnaires were mainly completed by the heads of sixth forms, from their perspective if their sixth forms were recruiting well, as they largely were, it would seem that the Year 11 post-16 guidance curriculum was doing its job. It is likely that heads of careers and careers service officers would have been less sanguine about the adequacy of the information and guidance provided to students in Year 11.

Dimensions of Choice 1: Staying in full-time education, getting a job or entering youth training

We have described and analysed the phenomena of increased staying-on rates in full-time education since the late 1980s in Chapters 1 and 2 and do not intend to labour the point here. But in our interviews with staff and students we asked for their explanations for the increased staying-on rates (staying-on rates in most of the schools had increased roughly in line with the local norms). Several interrelated explanations were offered. By far the most common was the general effect of lack of jobs for 16 year olds and the tough competition for jobs for older candidates. The widespread belief among students was that more and better qualifications would give an edge in the labour market. One Year 11 student said:

> People of my parents' generation could leave and get a decent job but it's not like that now, you've got to stay on and make the best of yourself otherwise you won't get the career you want. A lot of students are very career minded now.

We certainly found that a lot of the students we talked to were very career minded, although whether more so than in the past is a moot point. Many students certainly had a clear view of the labour market as difficult and highly competitive, in which only those with qualifications could expect to succeed. Some injected a note of scepticism, recognising the danger of qualifications inflation and commented that even being a graduate did not guarantee a good job any longer. But the overall attitude was that it was better to stay-on and hope that it would give an advantage when entering the labour market at a later time.

The effective option to staying-on, entering Youth Training, was largely discounted by the students. Taylor (Taylor, 1992) found that across all the schools in her study there was limited information about YT and that attitudes amongst students were mainly ignorant and hostile. YT was very much a last option for most students despite the fact that in Surrey at the time she conducted her research there were a significant number of placements offering employee status. As she points out these findings cast doubt on the rationale underpinning the introduction of training credits. Our data strongly reinforce her findings. In the majority of schools students appear to have been told little or nothing about YT. Where they had been they were not impressed. One sixth former said: 'YT is a bit of a joke, there's a lot of mickey-taking about it, that has destroyed its image.' In another school, although the students had not been told anything about YT, some had their own ideas: 'I think it's for if you don't know what you want to do.' Another student added: 'I heard about it because I have quite a few friends who did YT in different things, one of them left and the other doesn't really enjoy it.'

In another school information was provided on a differentiated basis. The top band Year 11 students we interviewed had been: 'Told virtually nothing about schemes, they might have skimmed over it in a careers lesson'. In contrast: 'Lower and middle band got a lot more, they were told about training credits, we weren't told about them at all.'

In one school a student had been on a YT course before deciding to return to school. He was scathing in his comments:

> The YT course was really poor, I went on it to earn a bit of money. It was pathetic, it looked as though the brainless were on it, some of

them were proper...nobody was bothered about them as long as they got paid for them being there. It was cheap labour, just giving you something to keep you busy.

These comments were indicative of the low esteem in which YT was held by the great majority of students, although most of them knew little about the scheme or had ever considered it something they may wish to do. Many schools ignored it completely or gave minimal information. Where students received any information it was most likely to come from careers service officers. Only a couple of schools appear to have adopted a more positive tone. We met only a handful of students among the more than 200 we interviewed who had seriously considered entering YT. There were echoes of an earlier time when one of these students told us how he had been encouraged by his parents to go onto YT as this 'would give him something to fall back on'.

The reputation of YT and its predecessors YOPS and YTS among students has always been shaky and the 'cheap labour' jibe could easily have come from the early 1980s rather than a decade later. But what is interesting is that whereas a decade ago a substantial number of 16 year olds were going on YTS schemes, the numbers have dwindled very considerably and very many youngsters who ten years ago would have gone on schemes now choose to stay-on in full-time education. It is as though the criticisms which have been made of the various youth training schemes have finally, after a lag of some ten years, impacted upon the behaviours of 16 year olds.

Some students and staff suggested that more people stayed-on in full-time education because they lacked the independence to get out into the 'real world'. One head of sixth commented: 'Increasingly we're finding that Year 11 pupils lack the confidence to move on in the way they have done in the past and that they actually need, many of them, to stay-on at school and develop their confidence.' A sixth former said: 'If you stay-on you can stay at home, you've got people looking after you and you're not expected to pay your way.' While another in another school claimed: 'Some people just want to stay-on at school for as long as they can, they don't want responsibility.'

It would be wrong, however, to portray the increase in staying-on as being solely due to the absence of a better alternative. Several students recognised that provision in sixth forms and colleges had diversified and there were more courses available. Greater publicity about the options and encouragement from schools and careers officers was also thought to have encouraged staying-on. Post-16 providers are now putting much greater efforts into recruiting students and this has encouraged more 16 year olds to stay-on. GCSE results had also improved which meant more people were eligible to stay-on. The overall attitude of many students was that school was OK, particularly in the sixth form with its more adult atmosphere of common rooms, social events and absence of school uniform. They could drop the subjects they did not like and concentrate on those they liked. The alternatives were not attractive and they hoped that the qualifications they expected to gain would give them an edge in a tough and competitive labour market.

In conclusion, it is evident that there were mixed motivations for staying-on in full-time education. There was some support for the notion that there has been a real change in culture among 16 year olds in relation to staying-on. One teacher at an inner city school put it thus:

> Whereas in the past the first thing they had in their minds when they got to Year 11 was to get out of school at 16 and get a job, that doesn't seem to fill their minds as much as it did. So something has happened there which is perhaps outside the culture of the school.

A head of sixth in another school offered a more localised explanation for a change in culture in his school:

> There are definitely increased horizons in this area. When I started here in 1980 the area was very introspective, but with the decline of the pits from 1984 new companies have come in and there has been an influx of outsiders. Students now have greater expectations. They're a lot more mobile, they used to think Wakefield was a million miles away. A lot more students drive now, a lot more have part-time jobs so they can combine school and work, earn some money which leaves them comfortably off, certainly far more than they could get on YT. There are no simplistic answers to why more are staying-on, it's a combination of a lot of things.

A deputy head in another school claimed: 'Youngsters are more and more willing to accept staying-on as normal practice. There's a threshold point after which it becomes much more the norm to stay-on. There's also greater parental support for staying-on'.

It seems to us that there are real grounds for suggesting that an important cultural shift has taken place and that this, in combination with the shift from an élite to a mass system of higher education, may be one of the most significant social changes of the 1990s. It might be that in the mid-1990s even the successors to Paul Willis' 'lads' (Willis, 1977) might stay-on at school to do their GNVQ Foundation or Intermediate level course, although whether at the end of it they would get anything other than 'working class jobs' is much more doubtful.

Dimensions of Choice 2: Staying at school or going to college

We asked both Year 11 students and sixth formers how they had decided or thought they would decide whether to stay-on at school or go to college. In choosing between school and college an interesting set of beliefs about colleges was revealed. Colleges were widely perceived as being more easygoing, providing less pastoral support and less discipline than schools. In college, many students thought, you were left to sink or swim. One sixth former said: 'College is better for people who are motivated and enthusiastic. This year I had a real problem getting motivated, if I'd been at college I'd have messed it up, so school's been good for that.' College was perceived as rather frightening. Sixth formers in another school said: 'It's just easier staying at school, I know it sounds really lazy, but it's daunting going to college.' Another added: 'I think I'd feel intimidated by college, all those people I don't know.'

Students in another school also had ideas of what the teaching was like in colleges:

People say it's harder at college, you just get lectured at college, it's not like a classroom environment and the teachers don't help you that much. That's what my parents have told me and the careers service and friends who've been to college.

In contrast to the harsh, impersonal world of the college, schools were seen as cosy, friendly environments which would also provide the firm discipline and guidance which students saw themselves as requiring. Three students commented: 'You're more confident of yourself at school, the teachers know you, they know what you're like and what you're good at, they help you more.' 'I'd just be lost at college.' 'It's not as strict at college, school teachers are always checking up on you and that's a good thing if you want to get somewhere.'

It must be stressed that our evidence is drawn from sixth formers and is by definition from those who chose not to go to college. Had we interviewed college students it is likely that we would have met some students who were only too ready to exchange college for school. However, it is evident that among school students there was a powerful mythology about life in colleges in which they were compared unfavourably with schools, although some students self-critically assumed that the problem lay with them rather than the colleges and that they lacked the maturity or self-discipline which they assumed was needed to cope within the college environment. There were exceptions among the students and we met some Year 11 students who were planning to leave school and go to college, who felt that they could handle the college environment and who saw positive advantages such as a more adult atmosphere and the chance to mix with a more heterogeneous student population. In general, however, there were strong normative pressures to stay on at school in a familiar environment, among friends and with familiar teachers. It is interesting to speculate where these perceptions of colleges came from. As we show below, in many schools students were given only limited information about colleges. Occasionally students claimed to have been explicitly discouraged from going to college by a teacher or careers officer and some teachers concurred with students' evaluation of colleges. For example a deputy head at one school said:

> Youngsters from this area don't flock to the city centre, if they feel comfortable at school they will stay here, they have a relationship with the school, it's a big step for them to go to college. Also the college response is totally cost-effective, their courses will only run if they enrol enough students. We don't function in the same way, we try to serve a need, we commit ourselves to running a particular course and stay with it whereas a college will just cut a course which is not economically viable.

The contrast drawn between the caring, community-centred school and the commercially driven college is transparent (although we have no evidence that the deputy head transmitted his opinion to students). In general it seemed that students derived their views of colleges from gossip among their friends and acquaintances, and the rather limited information most received about colleges was not enough to convince them to abandon the school, which they knew, for the unfamiliar college.

In the competitive post-16 student market colleges clearly have a big task to overcome the sort of student attitudes which our research revealed. We have already seen that there have been complaints from colleges about 11–18 schools denying their students information about colleges. In January 1994 the DfE wrote to all secondary schools and city technology colleges drawing their attention to new regulations which required them to pass on to their pupils information about the qualifications obtained by students in local further education colleges and the career routes they went on to take (*DfE News* 11/94).

However, by no means all the allegations of sharp practice in the recruitment of students post-16 have been aimed at schools. There have also been complaints nationally about the behaviour of some colleges in the competition for students. The September 1995 enrolment period brought media stories about colleges allegedly 'bribing' high achieving students with offers of 'scholarships.' A headteacher in one of the schools we visited complained about an aggressive newspaper, TV and radio advertising campaign, which he claimed contained anti-school messages, run by the local college which was able to employ a full-time marketing manager. In the Leeds area a pamphlet published in Autumn 1995 by the Leeds Colleges of Further Education and distributed free of charge to 310,000 homes, businesses, libraries, community and job centres used full page advertisements to exhort potential students: 'Don't be a sheep – do your own thing at Leeds Colleges of Further Education' and with a jokey reference to Robbie Williams, ex-member of Take That, advised students: 'Hey Robbie! We know why you left – and we know where you're going!' Such advertising will not be seen as in any way unfair by many, and from the market perspective is all part of the attempt to bring choice and diversity to students. But it was found distasteful by some in the schools and was certainly part of the phenomena of marketing and publicity which legislative changes have brought to schools and colleges in the 1990s. Critics of the new competition for students post-16 worried that, contrary to the claims that it brought diversity and choice, it in fact often served the interests of students poorly by denying them disinterested advice and surrounding their choices at post-16 with hype and publicity.

We asked sixth formers to assess the adequacy and fairness of the information they had received in Year 11 about other schools and colleges. No students had received information about other schools and the few students we met who had changed schools at 16 had sought out information for themselves. Interestingly, while school teachers seem to accept competition with colleges and independent schools as legitimate, or at least as a necessary evil, 'poaching' from state schools is resisted. There appears to be an unwritten convention among 11–18 schools that they do not compete for each other's students. The deputy head of one school made this explicit:

...we do vigorously attempt to recruit sixth formers in the community, hopefully not from neighbouring schools, God forbid that we should be pinching from [school] or [school] because that's the kind of battle that none of us ever want to get involved in....Personally I would hate to see people from [school] come here, that's the kind of dog fight we don't want to get into.

This is an interesting example of resistance to the culture of competition which government policy is eager to encourage. From a free market perspective it is difficult to see why schools should not wish to get into a dog fight? Why would a deputy head hate to see people from another school transferring to his school? This looks suspiciously like a local cartel distorting the market!

One sixth former was candid when asked to reflect upon the adequacy and fairness of information supplied in Year 11 about other schools and colleges offering post-16 courses:

> I thought it wasn't really adequate and it wasn't very fair [laughter]. Here we got the sixth form prospectus and a book about our school, you had to go out to other schools and get information, we didn't get anything about them or the college. We weren't encouraged to look at other places, the school assumed a natural progression into the sixth form.

Another member of the group supported this statement: 'It was a sort of natural progression into the sixth form, I didn't really think about the options, they weren't highlighted to us by the teachers.' The head of sixth form in this school commented: 'The competitive situation has made us much more aware of the need to recruit more positively but at the same time give objective and honest advice to Year 11 students.'

A common assessment was made by a sixth former in another school: 'The school itself didn't give us information about colleges, really it was left to us, if we wanted to change we had to ring them up and find out about open days and information days.' We put this assessment to the head of sixth in this school and asked if she thought it was fair:

> It is to an extent. It's not my job....I've got enough on telling them about what we do here without telling them about what other places do, but I think that they do get that perspective to a degree from the careers service and if they wanted to go off and do a vocational course we would advise them about where they might be able to go. But yes, it's in our interests to push our own sixth form, but that's not to say it hinders them in any way, they're at liberty to go and check out other places, they're not actively prevented from doing that.

There was support in our data for the head of sixth form's claim that the careers service provided another 'perspective' and for many students the individual interviews with careers officers were important sources of information about courses and institutions. The careers service was able to act as an 'honest broker' (to the annoyance of some teachers in at least one school, see page 104) although many students also said that they did not get much information and as many had only one interview lasting 15 to 20 minutes this was inevitable. It was clear that the information received from careers officers did not counterbalance that which the schools themselves were able to supply.

There is much in our data which supports complaints from colleges that in 11–18 schools students receive little or no information about what is available elsewhere. Unsurprisingly there was little recognition in the schools that this was a problem which needed tackling. One head of sixth however was unusually candid and radical in his response which is worth quoting at some length:

School staff should *not* be allowed to counsel students re post-16 possibilities! They cannot help but be biased towards academic routes, particularly, but not exclusively, if the school has a sixth form of its own. I advocate the intervention of a separate unbiased body. Currently this role is fulfilled by the careers service. One or two half-hour interviews in Year 11 is not nearly enough....The critical time is *Year 10*. Early in Year 11 decisions and applications have to be made. The emphasis must be placed on *independent, unbiased, individual counselling*, targeted mainly at *Year 10* but extending to Year 11. (Emphasis in original)

The candour and radicalism will be welcomed by many outside the schools but we suspect even our respondent would recognise that the changes he proposes are unlikely to occur. Even if they were to take place it is uncertain how much impact they would have. It was often the quiet word from a particular subject teacher or form tutor which seemed to have had an impact on individual students' decisions. It seems even less likely that the much less radical new regulations announced by the DfE in January 1994 will have a significant effect. It is unclear as to what would constitute 'passing-on' information about examination results and qualifications obtained in colleges. Distributing colleges' prospectuses to individual students? Making colleges' prospectuses available in careers libraries? Giving college staff direct access to Year 11 students through visits and participation in careers conventions and parents evenings? It is far from clear that even the most comprehensive package of these possibilities would compensate for the advantage which schools have of day-to-day contact with their pupils.

However, while accepting that there was much in our data which supported the complaints made by colleges, there were ameliorating factors. First, by no means all schools denied students information about colleges. In one school a sixth former said: 'It was fair because at the open evening people from different colleges were here so everybody had a chance to show what they could offer.' In another school a Year 11 student said: 'You're given a chance to find out about other places, no one says you're a criminal if you want to leave.' In a third school a student commented: 'There's no pressure to come back here, there are lots of prospectuses upstairs about colleges.' Another member of the group added: 'The teachers ask you why you want to come back, if you're not just taking the easy option, they ask you why you don't want to go to college.'

In another school we were told that:

I talked with quite a few teachers, they didn't pressurise me at all to stay at school, they said the decision was up to me, they gave me lots of information on grants, loans and training credits. We had an open day when we were told about colleges and we had a chance to visit some of the colleges, we were given the prospectuses in careers lessons and we also went to a careers convention where the colleges were represented.

Thus there was a significant minority of schools which provided information which the students we talked to judged to be fair and adequate about alternative post-16 institutions. A second factor was that even in those schools where the information was judged to be unfair and/or inadequate, some students recognised what was happening. One Year 11 student said: 'We'll have it drummed into us that it's better to stay-on here because of the money they'll get. We'll get a lot of information about the sixth form.' In another school a Year 11 student said: 'The information in school about other places has been reasonable, they tell you it's there, you can't expect them to sell it.'

Some parents, at least, were also aware of the pressures on schools. One Year 11 student told us how she had considered changing to another school because of what she and her parents saw as poor exam results. She had approached the careers teacher in the school and had been given 'fairly limited' information. Her father, however, had discounted this on the grounds that the teacher 'was bound to look after his own interests'. They had visited neighbouring school sixth forms but in the end had decided it would be best if she continued in her present school.

Finally, some students were able to use their own resources to seek out information on alternatives. In one school where students were agreed that they received little information, a Year 11 student told us how she had sought out information on the course she wanted to do:

I went to an open evening at one of the local colleges. I got a lot of leaflets and read quite a bit about GNVQs. But the best course for what I want to do is not a GNVQ, it's BTEC Travel and Tourism, it's the last year they're running it because GNVQ is coming in. I found out by going over there and looking around, I liked the place, the course sounds good, I've been over there for a day already. I prefer the BTEC course to GNVQ because you can choose different units, it seems to have more units than the GNVQ.

Another member of the same group was also going to college:

I got information about the college from the careers officer who told me about the place, so I went over and had a look around. I've also been for interviews to two other colleges, I passed those as well, so it was just where I wanted to go really, which place was better.

So students and their parents should not be thought of as dupes who lack the resources to find out for themselves about alternative sources of post-16 provision. Even among our skewed sample (i.e. those post-16 students who had stayed-on in school) there were those who had recognised when they were being supplied with inadequate or biased information and who had been proactive and researched the alternatives for themselves. However, rather as with the wider issue of parental choice in education, it is true that exercising choice at post-16 draws upon differentially available economic and cultural resources (Ball, Bowe and Gewirtz, 1994).

To conclude this section, our evidence supports other research findings which have suggested that there is a problem in the provision of unbiased advice about post-16 options in many 11–18 schools. This was thoroughly predictable and springs from the competitive position in which schools find themselves. The ambiguities inherent in this situation were well expressed by a deputy head:

I don't know what kind of subliminal pressures are operating through classrooms to encourage people to come back here, but our up front attitude through assemblies and through the careers programme is neutral, to use your word. On the other hand we have to accept the reality of the financial situation that sixth formers are enormously valuable to our retaining our staffing and we do vigorously attempt to recruit sixth formers in the community....We do say that we think we have a peerless A level set-up, with no consortium arrangements and so on, which I think don't work. So I do stand at the front and sell the widest range of A levels in any local school, all offered on site. By the same token I do stand there and say there's no pretending we can offer vocational courses on the scale that colleges can, or that we can offer hardware or facilities available there, so I hope there's a little bit of honesty each way.

For market theorists, no doubt, the absence of neutral unbiased information and guidance about post-16 options is seen as distorting the market. It is difficult to see what can be done about this. The government can regulate, as it has done, and the careers service can offer disinterested advice, but it seems unlikely that these strategies can compensate for the in-built 'subliminal pressures' available to schools. However, we think it important not to exaggerate the effects of these distortions on the actual destinations of students at post-16. It seems to us that even were every school to offer comprehensive and fair advice on the options available the numbers of students leaving 11–18 schools for other schools or colleges would be unlikely to increase dramatically. The lure of a familiar environment, often closer to home than the alternatives and the presence of friends and accustomed teachers is likely to persuade most post-16 students in schools with sixth forms that their most rational choice is to continue their full-time education at the school where they took their GCSEs.

Dimensions of Choice 3: Courses of study

There were two levels to choices of courses of study. One concerned selection of which track – academic or vocational – or combination of tracks to follow. The second related to the selection of courses within the tracks – which A or AS level subjects or vocational areas should be studied. We will consider first the choice of tracks and then examine the selection of courses within the tracks.

Vocational or academic courses?

The attempt to establish parity of esteem between academic and vocational courses claimed to be at the same level clearly has important implications for the guidance processes in Year 11. We were interested in the extent to which this assertion of parity of esteem was actually reflected in the practice in the schools. In particular we were interested in seeing how the new Advanced GNVQ courses were presented to students. Were they presented as courses which might be taken by the most academically able students? Or were they seen as second best for those who might not quite be up to A level?

These questions have been substantially addressed in Chapter 6 and thus will not be laboured here. Our research confirmed the findings of Alison Wolf and her colleagues in their National Survey Report on GNVQs 1993/94 (FEU, Institute of Education and Nuffield Foundation, 1994) that with regard to Advanced GNVQ there is a gap between schools' stated and actual recruitment practices. The majority of the school prospectuses refer to the alleged equivalency of an Advanced GNVQ to two GCE A levels and most schools ask for four or five GCSEs at grade C or above and thus make no distinction between entry requirements for Advanced GNVQ and most A level courses. One school for example described the course as 'A genuine alternative to A level', while another prospectus advised students: 'Don't dismiss them as inferior to A levels. The style of learning and assessment may suit you better.' The Manor Park case study (see page 22) illustrated the ways in which some schools designed their prospectuses in order to emphasise the equivalency between Advanced GNVQ and A levels. However, as was made clear in Chapter 6, when it came to actually counselling students as to which courses to take schools generally continued to advise those with the best GCSE results to follow A level courses. We found few students who had made a deliberate choice to take GNVQ rather than A level. The National Survey Report on GNVQs 1993/94 stated:

> In practice, Advanced GNVQ cohorts have up to now been markedly different from GCE A level ones....While there is some overlap, the GCE A level population is drawn mostly from the 'top' group of students in terms of GCE results and the GNVQ Advanced population from the middle range of GCSE achievement.
>
> (FEU, Institute of Education and Nuffield Foundation, 1994, p33)

Our evidence on the advice and guidance which was being offered to students suggests that there is unlikely to be much change in this situation. A number of factors contributed towards this state of affairs. A level courses were widely seen by teachers, students and, allegedly, parents as having high status. Partly as a consequence of this for students aiming for higher education, A levels were seen as a 'safe bet' whereas GNVQs were still something of an unknown quantity despite the encouraging noises which emanated from higher education institutions. A further factor was that GNVQs were seen to require a degree of vocational commitment from students which many were not ready to make. Despite its alleged narrowness A level was seen by many students as being something which you could take if you had only vague ideas of what your future career might be.

At Intermediate level the context was rather different. Stated entry requirements varied more than for Advanced level. Most commonly schools asked for 'a clutch of Ds' at GCSE level, but some had lower entry requirements. One school asked for three GCSEs at E or above plus a G in Maths and English. Another school asked for a D in English and Maths but no others asked for specific qualifications in the National

Curriculum core subjects. One school stated there was no formal requirement for entry to Intermediate GNVQ courses. The prospectuses gave less emphasis to equivalencies with academic courses than was the case at Advanced level but in about half the schools there was reference to equivalence to four or five GCSEs at grades A–C. In practice we found that many schools were operating a virtual open access policy with regard to Intermediate GNVQs. There was wide recognition that this was unsatisfactory because some students were struggling to cope with the courses but there was an absence of any alternative provision. In this respect many teachers recognised that Intermediate GNVQ was not a direct replacement for CPVE or even the more vocationally specific and rigorous DVE courses. Several schools looked forward to the introduction of Foundation GNVQ as filling the gap which had been left.

The liberal entry policies for Intermediate GNVQs also promised to have consequences for future recruitment to Advanced GNVQs. Several prospectuses indicated that achievement of an Intermediate GNVQ would satisfy the entry criteria for Advanced GNVQ. Some specified that this should be at merit or distinction level but most did not and this is again in line with the findings of the national survey (FEU, Institute of Education and Nuffield Foundation, 1994). The national survey also showed that many Intermediate level students intend to continue to Advanced level and then hope to enter higher education. This scenario suggests that not only will the three year post-16 course become more common but that a significant number of students will be completing, or at least entering, Advanced level courses and yet have only modest GCSE qualifications (including perhaps only grades G in Maths and English in the case of one school in our study). There was little or no evidence from our research that in their guidance programmes schools were making students aware of the possible implications of this situation. Of course it may be that higher education institutions will accept the achievement of a merit or distinction at Advanced GNVQ as an acceptable entry requirement even with moderate GCSE results but this is by no means certain. It also remains to be seen if achievement of an Intermediate GNVQ is adequate preparation for Advanced GNVQ.

Subjects for study?

Some students had definite career intentions which guided their choice of subjects post-16. For A level students intentions to go into medicine or engineering, for example, dictated the choice of at least some of their subjects. Generally though A level students were not strongly committed to specific careers, although they might have vague ideas of the general occupational fields in which they hoped to work. Indeed for students one of the advantages of A levels compared to GNVQs was that they did not require the same degree of vocational commitment. When asked why they had chosen particular A level subjects the great majority of students replied that they were subjects which they 'enjoyed' and/or 'were good at' and in which they had achieved GCSE grades A–C. We saw in Chapter 3 that many students found the transition from GCSE to A level difficult and some criticised the schools for not providing greater guidance on what to expect, the transition, they suggested, was presented as a 'natural progression'. Some teachers accepted that there was some validity in these criticisms but suggested that attempts to warn students about the difficulty of the transition often fell on deaf ears. Both teachers and students agreed that the most effective guidance often came from current sixth formers and some schools made formal arrangements for existing sixth formers to talk to prospective sixth formers. While schools probably could do more to prepare students for the transition to A level, it seems to us that this is essentially a curricular issue rather than one of guidance.

A few students chose Advanced GNVQ on the basis of a definite vocational commitment. One of these said:

> I've had people asking me 'Why are you doing BTEC when you got such good grades?' They don't understand that that's what I wanted to do and it's all I was interested in. I could have done any of the A levels but I was interested in business and the school didn't offer any courses around business, I want a career somewhere in business.

Students with this degree of vocational commitment were rare among GNVQ candidates as well as among those opting for A levels. Most students entering GNVQ courses had done so because they had not achieved the GCSE grades required to take an A level course but wanted to stay on in full-time education. Having decided to remain at school rather than college they were then left to select from the usually rather limited range of vocational courses on offer. It would be putting it too strongly to suggest that students had drifted into GNVQ courses, but many of them appeared to have been required to make a greater degree of vocational commitment than they were ready to make. One criticism of current national provision may be that it lacks a true pre-vocational alternative, although heads of sixth forms were somewhat divided upon how much demand there would be for such a course and some thought that GNVQ was sufficiently broad in its approach to be able to cater for the vast majority of student needs.

Concluding comments

Guidance and counselling in schools on post-16 options has been heavily criticised in recent times both by government agencies and colleges. The tenor of some of this criticism is that many of the problems post-16 are the products of inadequate guidance pre-16 and the consequent failure to match students to courses and that if only these failings could be corrected many of the problems would disappear. Our own account in this chapter also has something of a similar flavour. But there is an element of injustice in this criticism which should also be acknowledged. We must recognise the contexts within which guidance on post-16 options takes place.

First, it occurs within an overcrowded Key Stage 4 curriculum in which the National Curriculum and school performance tables placed the emphasis on attainment in GCSE examinations. When the longer-standing problems of staffing and training for careers education and guidance are added to this it can be appreciated that schools face severe difficulties in achieving the quantity and quality of guidance which they desire.

Second, recent government policy has placed schools in a competitive relationship to other post-16 providers. This is not something which most schools sought and it is a source of regret for many, but having been placed in that situation schools can hardly be blamed, nor should anyone be surprised, if they use the advantages of their position to promote their own post-16 offerings at the expense of their competitors. However, this tendency should not be exaggerated. We found that some schools did give fair and adequate advice on provision elsewhere. Nor should it be assumed that were such practices to be universal it would have a major impact on the actual destinations of students post-16 since there might be very good reasons for most students to continue their full-time education in the schools where they took their GCSEs.

Third, there is implied criticism of the ways in which schools have guided students with respect to GNVQs. Many have advised the brightest academic students to take A levels rather than GNVQs (although we have little evidence that many of these students ever contemplated taking GNVQs anyway). This is clearly an impediment to the achievement of parity of esteem by Advanced GNVQs, an aim with which many teachers were sympathetic. This was an example of a type of conflict familiar to many teachers in which their educational ideals clashed with what they saw as their responsibility to individual students. While they may have been sympathetic to GNVQs, when it came to advising individual students many teachers advised them to follow A level courses if they could, and given the novel character of GNVQs and the question marks which have been raised about them, it would be a brave critic who would assert that the advice given by these teachers under these circumstances was wrong.

With Intermediate GNVQs schools have been criticised for their over-liberal entrance policies and yet in the absence of any clear-cut alternative courses for those students wishing to continue in full-time education it is difficult to see what else teachers could have done. Many recognised the problems but were not responsible for the absence of nationally recognised courses for those for whom neither A levels nor Advanced and Intermediate GNVQs were suitable (a more valid criticism of guidance in schools may be its neglect of YT as an appropriate route for some youngsters).

Fourth, schools may be criticised for their neglect of systematic use of information on the predictive powers of GCSE results in guiding post-16 choices. There is some validity in this criticism, but as we saw in Chapter 3 predicting performance post-16 on the basis of attainment at GCSE is by no means straightforward. Indeed the evidence of the various studies suggests that the general strategy adopted by most schools of flexibility and sensitivity to individuals' needs is hard to fault. Of course, in particular schools and with individual students, this general strategy might be imperfectly applied and be subject to all sorts of distortions, but the overall approach adopted in most schools seems to us to be a reasonable response to the available information and the conditions under which they operate.

Our general conclusion is that we should be cautious in attributing too many of the problems, particularly in relation to non-completion and non-success rates on post-16 courses, to the guidance provided pre-16. In a sense pre-16 guidance is an easy target in the search for solutions to post-16 problems – leaving the more difficult issues of status differentials between courses and curricular progression still to be tackled.

CHAPTER 9

Whither 16–19 Education and Training?

Education and training for 16–19 year olds is characterised by both change and continuity. Over the last decade there have been great changes in vocational qualifications and courses, school and college organisational structures and funding arrangements. The continuity has been provided by the academic curriculum and particularly the A level label which continues to be the bedrock of the curriculum and provides the yardstick against which other courses and qualifications are measured. In many ways the debate about the 16–19 curriculum reflects wider tensions within Conservative policy on the curriculum between modernisers and traditionalists (see for example Ball, 1990; Jones, 1989). The challenge for Conservative policy is to produce a 16–19 education system which can provide access, increase participation and promote learning experiences which will contribute to economic regeneration and at the same time preserve A levels in all their 'rigour'.

However, despite the government's steadfast defence of the multi-track system which it has created, one of the features of the debate on the 16–19 curriculum has been the emergence of a broad consensus in favour of change. As we saw in Chapter 1 a number of influential organisations have come out in favour of greater flexibility, coherence and breadth often involving modularisation and credit transfer in the curriculum. Perhaps the most remarkable of all the calls for reform was the Joint Statement issued by six school and college organisations (AfC/GSA/HMC/SHA/APVIC/SHMIS, 1994). This called for academic and vocational qualifications to be brought together within a single national qualification composed of units of assessment which might be academic or vocational in origin and which could be combined horizontally and vertically to ensure breadth and depth appropriate to the needs of students. As the signatories to this statement included the GSA, HMC and SHMIS it was difficult for it to be represented as a flight of fancy of the trendy-left educational establishment. Even for a government which has been as disdainful as this one of education professionals the weight of opinion in favour of reform was difficult to ignore and it was this which almost certainly prompted the government to ask Sir Ron Dearing to review the framework of 16–19 qualifications.

Dearing issued his interim report in July 1995 with the full report scheduled to be published in April 1996 (Dearing, 1995). Although the interim report left a good many questions open it clearly indicated the directions of Sir Ron's thoughts on the issues to be included in the final report. We will highlight here those which are of particular relevance to the issues discussed in this book. Before doing this, however, it is necessary to refer briefly to Dearing's terms of reference for the review because these constrained any proposals he was likely to make. His terms of reference reflected the tension between change and continuity. On the one hand, he was asked specifically to 'have particular regard to the need to maintain the rigour of General Certificate of Education (GCE) Advanced (A) levels' and 'continue to build on the current development of General National Vocational Qualifications (GNVQs) and National Vocational Qualifications (NVQs).' The emphasis on the maintenance of rigour needs little elaboration while reference to the three separate tracks within the existing system clearly indicated that the creation of a unified system was not to be on Dearing's agenda. Further terms of reference however, gave him some room for manoeuvre. He was asked: 'Is there scope for measures to achieve greater coherence and breadth of study post-16 without compromising standards; and how can we strengthen our qualifications framework further?' Another question posed was: 'And should we encourage core skills, which are already an essential part of GNVQs, as part of the programmes of study for more 16 to 19 year olds?' The appearance of the old favourites breadth, coherence and core skills gave Dearing the chance to go beyond the simple affirmation of the separate academic and vocational tracks implied elsewhere in the terms of reference and he seized this opportunity in the interim report in ways which were widely welcomed. Gillian Shephard described the report as 'an excellent stepping stone to the next stage of the review' while representatives of SHA, National Association of Head Teachers (NAHT), Association of Principals of Sixth Form Colleges (APSFC), AfC and the Association of Teachers and Lecturers (ATL) also supported the report using phrases such as 'delighted', 'very exciting' and 'strongly supported'. The CBI's director of education and training thought the report 'very positive' in identifying issues which needed to be tackled. David Blunkett for the Labour Party claimed that Sir Ron had recognised what his party had long been saying about the need for greater breadth of experience in the academic and vocational. The only slight note of discord came from Liberal Democrat education spokesman Don Foster who accused Dearing of having got 'cold feet' and only offering 'half a loaf' instead of the full integration of academic and vocational qualifications which his party advocated (*TES*, 21 July 1995).

Dearing achieved this remarkable degree of consensus in responses to the report by steering a characteristically skilful course between the modernisers and the traditionalists. Most people with views on the 16–19 curriculum could take heart from something in the review. For the traditionalists, Dearing was strong in his defence of A level and proposed various enquiries into possible variations in 'rigour' across subjects, examination boards and syllabus types. This was given added impetus by the annual furore which arose when the publication of A level results in August 1995 revealed that grades were continuing to improve, promoting suspicion in some quarters that this was evidence of falling standards (it was ironic that a decline in GCSE grades in maths and science was taken by some as evidence of falling standards there).

Dearing also offered something to those who favoured reform of academic and vocational qualifications and curricula. While he rejected the radical approach of sweeping away the current framework, he proposed that consideration should be given to the establishment of a 'common family of National Certificates giving details of the awards achieved and the name of the awarding bodies' (Dearing, 1995, p12). This, in essence, was a return to the idea of an Advanced Diploma mooted in the *Education and Training for the 21st Century* White Paper in 1991 but subsequently dropped. Dearing went further, however, in suggesting the creation of an award within the National Certificates which would accredit the achievement of both depth and breadth in Advanced level courses. He gave as an example of what might be required for such an award: the achievement of two full subjects at Advanced level, others at reformulated AS level plus the three core skills mandatory in GNVQ. He also suggested the possibility of grading groups of units in the GNVQ to provide the possibility of groups equal in size to A and AS levels. This would increase the coherence of the framework and encourage courses combining academic and vocational qualifications. Further suggestions included credit transfer between examining boards and pathways in 'closely related subject areas' and consultation with the Universities and Colleges Admissions Service (UCAS) on the feasibility of combining achievements in A levels and vocational qualifications into an overall numerical score.

On the issues of core skills and breadth Dearing hedged his bets. He recognised the importance attached to core skills, particularly by employers, and acknowledged that they were not included in all A level subjects but called for in-depth consideration of their inclusion in A level and NVQ programmes in the second part of the review. The interim report suggested the possibility of rewarding breadth with an additional award within the National Certificate, but came out against compulsory breadth of the kind proposed by the IPPR and the National Commission on Education. He recognised the failure of AS levels and proposed exploration of their reformulation as an intermediate qualification between GCSE and A level.

In essence while Dearing rejected the notion of a 'big bang' reform of 16–19 qualifications and curricula, he clearly favoured an incremental and evolutionary approach towards a more flexible framework which would enable combinations of vocational and academic qualifications, credit transfer and the establishment of an umbrella National Certificate covering the different tracks. The general tenor of his approach was against compulsion and regulation by central government. He favoured persuasion through the offering of additional certification as the means of creating more flexible and coherent patterns of participation, curricula and qualifications for 16–19 year olds. It seems likely that individual schools and colleges will continue to enjoy a good deal of autonomy in their provision of post-16 courses and options and this approach well accords with Dearing's review of the National Curriculum in which he restored a greater degree of flexibility to schools.

This flexible and enabling approach will undoubtedly win much support, especially in schools. Our research showed that there was a good deal of endorsement for change in the 16–19 curriculum in the directions suggested by most advocates of reform. Set against this, schools and colleges have been through an unprecedented period of change, certainly since 1988, and teachers are weary of innovation. It seems likely that further major imposed change would not be appreciated. Thus the chance, which seems likely to be offered by Dearing, to move at their own pace towards a more flexible and coherent post-16 curriculum will, we believe, be widely welcomed. Michael Young, a co-author of the IPPR Report *A British Baccalaureat* (Finegold et al, 1990), has recently argued that there is scope for bottom-up progress towards the sort of unified, modular curriculum advocated in that report (Young et al, 1994).

A further policy development which has the potential to help bridge the academic–vocational divide in curriculum was the merger of the Department for Education and the Employment Department to form the

Department for Education and Employment (DFEE) with Gillian Shephard as the first Secretary of State of the new 'super' department. This was a move which had long been advocated by many commentators on the education and training scene as being a prerequisite to bringing greater coherence to education and training provision. The National Commission on Education, for example, had proposed the creation of a Department for Education and Training (National Commission on Education, 1993). The timing of the change, however, caught many unawares and is difficult to account for other than in terms of internal Conservative party politics in the wake of Major's re-election as party leader. The merger was applauded by many involved in 16–19 education and training. Sir Geoffrey Holland, who had been a permanent secretary in both departments welcomed it as 'better late than never', but observed that the two departments were very different in style and that it was essential to effect real integration between them otherwise the change 'is not worth making'. In common with many others, Holland saw a principal potential advantage of the merger as the scope it presented for bringing about the 'long overdue integration of technical, vocational and academic programmes and qualifications' (*THES*, 14 July 1995).

Further examples of institutional convergence have been the moves by the vocational examining boards to establish closer links with the GCSE and GCE boards. The University of London Examinations and Assessment Council (ULEAC) and BTEC have already announced their intention to merge by the end of 1995. ULEAC is one of the largest GCSE and GCE examining boards while BTEC commands nearly 70 per cent of the market for GNVQs. The chief executives of the two examining bodies justified the proposed merger partly on the grounds that it would make it easier for students to 'pick and mix' combinations of GNVQs and A levels.

In the light of these mergers the continued separation of SCAA and NCVQ appears anachronistic and many expect these two bodies to be merged in the not too distant future. In September 1995 Education and Employment Minister, Lord Henley, announced a five yearly review of NCVQ. Part of this review would involve 'a study of the scope for privatising, contracting out any of the functions as well as possibilities for merger with or transferring some or all of NCVQ's functions to another body.' The government was committed to 'making sure that bodies like the Council remain in existence only when a real need can be demonstrated, and that they are performing as well as they possibly can' (*DFEE News* 194/95).

For those who favour reform of the 16–19 curriculum recent

developments have been relatively encouraging, although some would wish that Dearing had gone further. But it is worth injecting a note of caution. As Holland suggests mergers do not always bring about real integration and there are many examples, in education and elsewhere, where merged groups within institutions continue to pursue differing aims and objectives within ostensibly unified organisations. His point about the different styles of the DfE and the ED probably applies particularly strongly to SCAA and NCVQ, which in turn is reflected in the very different curricular, pedagogical and assessment characteristics of the courses for which each is responsible. Bringing these together, particularly when much emphasis is given to maintaining the 'rigour' of A levels will be no easy task. And while Dearing's incremental approach undoubtedly has much to commend it, the danger (for those who seek reform) is that it will not produce significant change. For example, although a National Certificate may be established, it remains to be seen whether the whole becomes more valued than the constituent parts. Would a National Certificate merely mask continued discrimination between academic and vocational components by 'users'? At a more general level we have to question the extent to which structural changes such as the creation of a new department, validating body or certificate can actually change deep-seated cultural values. There are good grounds for thinking that the distinctions made between academic and vocational courses are rooted in distinctions between mental and manual labour which are endemic in English culture. This is not to say that structural changes are irrelevant to deconstructing these distinctions and hence not worth making, but only that change is likely to be a long haul.

Following this brief discussion of aspects of the recent 'high politics' of 16–19 education and training we will end the book by briefly reviewing our own research and highlighting a few of the implications of our findings for the reform agenda. One feature which emerged was that there was tough competition for post-16 students in many localities. Many of the schools in our study were quickly coming to terms with the need to compete in the quasi-market created by recent legislation. Attracting students was a top priority and any future changes in the 16–19 curriculum will interact, in perhaps unpredictable ways, with this market context. Schools and colleges have of necessity to 'read' the local student market, and while it would be an exaggeration to suggest that this reading is the dominant factor in determining curriculum provision, it is something which schools and colleges cannot afford to ignore.

Unsurprisingly, A levels remained the dominant element of the curriculum in the schools (this is clearly one of the significant differences between schools and further education colleges). Many teachers were ambivalent in their attitudes to A level. Many agreed that A level courses were often unacceptably narrow in their content and rigid in their pedagogical and assessment procedures. And yet there was still a strong attachment to the high academic standards of the A level. For many teachers there remained a great deal of satisfaction to be gained from teaching an able, strongly motivated A level group. The view of A levels as moribund and encased in tradition was also shown to be simplistic. Where teachers wanted to carry on very much as before they could do, but there were new syllabuses and new approaches, sometimes involving modularisation and coursework, which could be adopted by teachers who wished to change the A level experience of students. Although the number of syllabuses makes generalisation difficult there has been a gradual process of change within the A level curriculum.

Students found A levels hard, sometimes stimulating and sometimes boring, most found the transition from GCSE difficult. It was notable that there was very little support from students for reform of the post-16 curriculum. For example, the prospect of imposed breadth filled many with horror, for them the narrowness of A level was a positive advantage. Of course, many teachers will recognise the innate conservatism of students and those we interviewed were mainly those who had succeeded within the existing system, but the resistance of students to the reform of the curriculum is something which we believe has been insufficiently taken account of by those who wish to bring about reform. This is not to say that a broader course with greater emphasis on core skills, for example, could not be made acceptable to a different cohort of students, but it does indicate that if the general principle of greater breadth post-16 is accepted there is still a major task of curriculum development to be undertaken. For example, where students already dislike maths, science or modern languages at GCSE level how would elements of these be made acceptable at post-16 if they were included as core elements of the curriculum?

Our research confirmed that AS levels have failed. They have not acted as a significant broadening element of the curriculum and have remained marginalised. Dearing's suggestion that they be reconstructed as an intermediate qualification clearly sounds their death knell in their current form. But we remain unsure about their function as an intermediate qualification. Are they there to provide breadth for those undertaking a standard three A level course, for those for whom A level is considered too hard or both? It is not clear that they will attract sufficient students to make them economically viable for many schools. We were told in many schools that it was not so much the concept of AS levels which was flawed as the practical difficulties of staffing and timetabling the courses. It is not immediately clear how AS, reborn as an intermediate qualification, will overcome these problems.

We traced the complex evolution of vocational courses in Chapters 5 and 6. The new dominant player here is GNVQ although claims for the 'success' of these new programmes by their advocates has been overstated. Since the government mandated that existing vocational courses had to be replaced by GNVQs they could hardly fail. Our research revealed a considerable expansion of the vocational curriculum in the schools so that about 25 per cent of students were following vocational courses. Inevitably at this stage in their development, the jury is still out on GNVQs and as we saw the early evaluations have been mixed. Despite this, the GNVQ bandwagon is rolling on, pulled vigorously by the NCVQ, with recent proposals to extend the model to HND and degree levels (*THES*, 15 September 1995) and is part of a wider movement to promote outcome focused approaches across a wide range of occupations and professions. Set alongside this expansionism, however, the government has responded to criticisms of GNVQs by attempting to inject more 'rigour' into their curriculum and assessment practices. At issue here is the extent to which this can be achieved while still retaining the original practical thrust of the qualifications. We noted in Chapter 6 that GNVQs are rather different from NVQs and are perceived by some as drifting towards the 'academic' and away from the concept of competence-based qualifications embodied in NVQs.

Core skills are back on the agenda in a big way through their inclusion in the terms of reference for the Dearing review. There is a strong sense of déjà vu here since similar processes of consultation and discussion took place in the late 1980s and yet came to very little, at least as far as academic courses were concerned. The strongest impression which emerges from our research is of the huge gap which exists between the aspirations of those who advocate core skills and the current practice in the schools. The timetabled core curricular provision which existed varied greatly and in most schools struggled for time, resources, commitment and status. It was invariably the main courses which counted for most with students and teachers. Our research was not designed to investigate the extent to which core skills were being achieved in main academic courses, but it is plausible to speculate that while at least elements of communication skills permeate academic courses the position with regard to numeracy and information technology is much more problematic. The mandatory inclusion and assessment of core skills at A level would likely require some major changes in many courses. As we noted above, in his interim report Dearing hedged his bets on these issues (Dearing, 1995, pp28–30). We await his final report with interest but suggest that a likely outcome is further consultation on the definition of core skills and the ways in which they can be taught and assessed.

Finally it is important to reiterate that amidst the many problematic features discussed above, the doubling of staying-on rates at 16 over the last decade has been remarkable. From being a minority pursuit staying-on has become the norm for many 16 year olds. It is important not to be complacent and staying-on rates at 17 and 18 are considerably lower than those at 16. We have also seen that in 1994/95 staying-on rates at 16 declined slightly for the first time in almost a decade. However, it seems to us this hardly warrants the description 'a new crisis' (see *THES*, 16 August 1995) and the overall pattern of the last decade is of unparalleled expansion. Indeed there is a danger of making a sacred cow of the full-time staying-on rate. It seems unlikely that staying-on in full-time education is the best option for all 16 year olds and the provision of good quality work-based training must remain an important priority for education and training policy. The modern apprenticeships scheme may go some way to meet this priority.

We would like to end this book where we began by stressing the crucial role of colleges, schools, teachers and students in making and re-making policy through implementation. Systems and structures are important, they provide the frameworks within which colleges, schools, teachers and students work but there is a danger of giving them too much emphasis. Ultimately the quality of 16–19 education and training depends upon the teaching and learning transactions which take place between students and teachers in classrooms, laboratories and workshops. This makes the achievement of real change both a more difficult and a more creative process. More difficult because it requires the participation of colleges, schools, teachers and students up and down the country, and more creative because it opens up the possibility of drawing upon the enthusiasm and expertise of education professionals and engaging them in a serious debate about the purposes of 16–19 education and training. There is great scope for developing bottom-up approaches to the reform of the 16–19 curriculum to complement the top-down perspectives of the systems builders. Our research brought us into contact with many thoughtful, clear-sighted teachers (and students) and we suggest that in planning ways forward for 16–19 education and training there is much to be gained through the involvement of practitioners both by giving them scope to develop curricula which are responsive to their local contexts and by giving them a voice in national debates on structures and frameworks.

References

AfC/GSA/HMC/SHA/APVIC/SHMIS (1994) *Post-Compulsory Education and Training*.

Ashford, S., Gray, J. and Tranmer, M. (1993) *The introduction of GCSE exams and changes in post-16 participation.* Sheffield: Employment Department.

Audit Commission/OFSTED (1993) *Unfinished Business: Full-time Educational Courses for 16–19 Year Olds.* London: HMSO.

Ball, S. (1990) *Politics and Policy Making in Education: Explorations in Policy Sociology.* London: Routledge.

Ball, S., Bowe, R. and Gewirtz, S. (1994) 'Market forces and parental choice: self-interest and competitive advantage in education', in Tomlinson, S. (ed.) *Educational Reform and its Consequences*, pp13–25. London: IPPR/Rivers Oram Press.

Barnes, D., Johnson, G., Jordan, S., Layton, D., Medway, P., Peacock, M. and Yeomans, D. (1989) *A Third Report on the TVEI Pilot Curriculum: courses for 16–18 year olds in sixteen local authorities.* Sheffield: Training Agency.

Boswell, T. (1994) *GCE qualifications and the new post-16 qualifications framework.* Text of a speech to the NEAB Conference 'The future of A-levels'. London: NEAB.

Burchell, H. (1992) 'Reforming the Advanced Level Curriculum', *Educational Studies,* **18**(1), 57–69.

CBI (1989) *Towards a Skills Revolution: Report of the Vocational Education and Training Task Force.* London: CBI.

CBI (1993) *Routes for success.* London: CBI.

Chapman, B. (1991) 'The overselling of science education in the eighties', School Science Review, **72**(260), 47–64.

Cleaton, D. (1993) *Careers Education and Guidance in British Schools.* Stourbridge: Institute of Careers Guidance.

Coates, P. (1991) 'The 16–19 core skills initiative', *The Curriculum Journal,* **2**(1), 43–53.

CEM (1994) *Comparing Examination Boards and Syllabuses at A-Level: students' grades, attitudes and perceptions of classroom processes.* NICCEA.

Cross, M. (1991) 'The Role of the National Council for Vocational Qualifications', in Chitty, C. (ed.) *Post-16 Education: Studies in Access and Achievement*, pp167–75. London: Kogan Page.

Dearing, R. (1995) *Review of 16–19 Qualifications.*

DES (1982) *17+, a New Qualification.* London: HMSO.

DES (1984) *AS Levels: Proposals by the Secretaries of State for Education and Science and Wales for a Broader Curriculum for A Level students.* London: HMSO.

DES (1986) *Broadening A Level Studies: Advanced Supplementary levels – a guide for schools and colleges.* London: HMSO.

DES (1988) *Advancing A Levels: Report of a Committee appointed by the Secretary of State for Education and the Secretary of State for Wales* (The Higginson Report). London: HMSO.

DES (1989) *Post 16 Education and Training, Core Skills: an HMI paper.* London: HMSO.

DES/DOE/Welsh Office (1991) *Education and Training for the 21st Century.* (White Paper). London: HMSO.

DfE (1994) 'Answers by the Department for Education to questions posed by the National Commission on Education', in National Commission on Education, *Insights into Education and Training*, pp297-322. London: Heinemann.

DfE (1995) *GCSE to GCE A/AS Value Added: Briefing for Schools and Colleges.* London: DfE.

DOE (1992) *Labour Market Skills and Trends 1993–94.* Sheffield: Employment Department.

DOE (1993) *Labour Market and Skills Trends 1994–95.* Sheffield: Employment Department Group.

DTI (1994) *Competitiveness: helping Business to Win.* (White Paper). London: HMSO.

DTI (1995) *Competitiveness: forging ahead.* (White Paper). London: HMSO.

FEFC (1994a) *General Certificate of Education Advanced Level and Advanced Supplementary Qualifications: National Survey Report.* London: FEFC.

FEFC (1994b) *GNVQs in Further Education in England.* London: FEFC.

FEU (1979) *A Basis for Choice.* London: FEU.

FEU (1992) *Core Skills in Action.* London: FEU.

FEU (1995) *A framework for credit: a common framework for post-14 education and training for the twenty-first century.* London: FEU.

FEU, Institute of Education and Nuffield Foundation (1994) *GNVQs 1993–94: a national survey report.* London: Further Education Unit/Institute of Education.

Finegold, D., Keep, E., Miliband, D., Raffe, D., Spours, K. and Young, M. (1990) *A British Baccalaureat: Ending the division between education and training.* London: IPPR.

Grint, K. (1991) *The Sociology of Work.* Cambridge: Polity Press.

Hall, V. (1994) *Further Education in the United Kingdom.* London: Collins

Educational.

Harrop, J. (1992) *Response to the Consultation on GNVQ: NCVQ Report No. 15*. London: NCVQ.

HMC (1993) *Education 14–19*. HMC.

HMI (1989) *GCE Advanced Supplementary Examinations: The first two years*. London: DES.

HMI (1990) *Survey of Guidance 13–19 in Schools and Sixth Form Colleges*. London: DES.

HMI (1992) *Evaluating Developments in Advanced Supplementary Examinations 1990–91*. London: DES.

Hodkinson, P. and Mattinson, K. (1994) 'A bridge too far? The problems facing GNVQ', *The Curriculum Journal*, 5(3), 323–36.

Hyland, T. (1994) *Competence, Education and NVQs: Dissenting Perspectives*. London: Cassell.

Hyland, T. (1995) 'GNVQs, VET and Comprehensive Education', *Forum*, 37(1), 14–5.

Jessup, G. (1991) *Outcomes: NVQs and the Emerging Model of Education and Training*. Lewes: Falmer Press.

Jones, K. (1989) *Right Turn: The Conservative Revolution in Education*. London: Hutchinson.

Kelly, A.V. (1990) *The National Curriculum: a critical review*. London: Paul Chapman Publishing.

Kerr, D. (1992) 'The Academic Curriculum – Reform Resisted', in Whiteside, T., Sutton, A. and Everton, T. (eds) *16–19 Changes in Education and Training*, pp42–53. London: David Fulton Publishers.

Kidd, L. (1991) *16–19: The Way Forward*. Leicester: Secondary Heads Association.

Kidd, L. (1992) *16–19: Towards a coherent system*. Leicester: Secondary Heads Association.

Lawson, T. (1992) 'Core Skills 16–19', in Whiteside, T., Sutton, A. and Everton, T. (eds) *16–19 Changes in Education and Training*, pp85–94. London: David Fulton Publishers.

McCulloch, G. (1989) *The Secondary Technical School: A Usable Past?* London: Falmer Press.

Macintosh, H. (1986) 'The Certificate of Pre-Vocational Education', in Ranson, S., Taylor, B. and Brighouse, T. (eds) *The Revolution in Education and Training*, pp89–99. York: Longman.

Moon, B. (1988) 'Introducing the Modular Curriculum to Teachers', in Moon, B. (ed.) *Modular Curriculum*, pp3–21. London: Paul Chapman Publishing.

National Commission on Education (1993) *Learning to Succeed*. London: Heinemann.

NCC (1990) *Core Skills 16–19: A response to the Secretary of State*. York: NCC.

NCVQ (1992) *NVQ Monitor*. London: NCVQ.

NCVQ (1994) *Annual Report 1993–94*. London: NCVQ.

166

NEAB (1995) *Towards a Single Qualifications System: Consultation on the Reform of A Levels.* Manchester: NEAB.

Oates, T. (1992) *Developing and Piloting the NCVQ Core Skills Units: an outline of method and a summary of findings.* London: NCVQ.

Oates, T. and Harkin, J. (1995) 'From Design to Delivery: the implementation of the NCVQ core skills units', in Burke, J. (ed.) *Outcomes, Learning and the Curriculum,* pp182–200. London: Falmer Press.

OCSEB (1994) *Diploma of Achievement: Prospectus.* OCSEB.

OFSTED (1992) *GNVQs in schools: The Introduction of General National Vocational Qualifications.* London: HMSO.

OFSTED (1993) *GCE Advanced Supplementary and Advanced Level Examinations.* London: HMSO.

OFSTED (1994) *GNVQs in Schools 1993–94.* London: HMSO.

Pring, R. (1994) 'Bridging the Academic/Vocational Divide'. Text of a speech to the NEAB Conference 'The future of A-levels'. London: NEAB.

Raffe, D. (1993a) 'Multi-track and unified systems of post-compulsory education and 'upper secondary education in Scotland': an analysis of two debates', *British Journal of Educational Studies,* **XXXXI**(3), 223–52.

Raffe, D. (1993b) 'Participation of 16–18 Year Olds in Education and Training', in *Briefings for the National Commission on Education,* pp31–45. London: Heinemann.

Rainbow, B. (1993) 'Modular A and AS Levels: the Wessex Project', in Richardson, W., Woolhouse, J. and Finegold, D. (eds) (1993) *The Reform of Post–16 Education and Training in England and Wales,* pp87–100. York: Longman.

Richardson, W., Woolhouse, J. and Finegold, D. (eds) (1993) *The Reform of Post–16 Education and Training in England and Wales.* York: Longman.

Sanderson, M. (1994) *The Missing Stratum: Technical School Education in England, 1900–1990s.* London: Athlone Press.

Schools Council (1966) *Sixth Form: Curriculum and Examinations.* London: HMSO.

SCAA (1993) SCAA post–16 team, *NAS Coursework* Briefing Note, December. London: SCAA.

SCAA (1995) *Using the Advanced Supplementary Examination.* London: SCAA.

SCAA and the GCE Examining Boards of England, Wales and Northern Ireland (1994) *Code of Practice for GCE A and AS Examinations.* London: SCAA.

SEAC (1990) *Examinations Post–16: Developments for the 1990s.* London: SEAC.

SEAC (1991) *Report on the Consultation of Draft Principles for GCE A and AS Examinations.* London: SEAC.

SEAC (1992) *Principles for GCE Advanced and Advanced Supplementary Examinations.* London: SEAC.

Smithers, A. (1993) *All Our Futures: Britain's Education Revolution.* London:

167

Channel Four Televison.

Smithers, A. (1994) 'The Paradox of A Levels', *The Curriculum Journal*, **5**(3), 355–63.

Smithers, A. and Robinson, P. (1993) *General Studies: breadth at A-level*. London: The Engineering Council.

Spours, K. (1991) 'The Politics of Progression: Problems and Strategies in the 14–19 Curriculum', in Chitty, C. (ed.) *Post-16 Education: Studies in Access and Achievement*, pp72–86. London: Kogan Page.

Spours, K. (1993) 'Analysis: the reform of qualifications within a divided system', in Richardson, W., Woolhouse, J. and Finegold, D. (eds) *The Reform of Post-16 Education and Training in England and Wales*, pp146–70. York: Longman.

Stanton, G. (1994) 'Post-16 Curriculum and Qualifications: Confusion and Incoherence or Diversity and Choice?', in National Commission on Education *Insights into Education and Training*, pp241–56. London: Heinemann.

Taylor, M. (1992) 'Post-16 options: young people's awareness, attitudes and influences in their choice', *Research Papers in Education*, **7**(3), 301–36.

Watkins, P. (1991) 'High Technology, Work and Education', in Dawkins, D. (ed.) *Power and Politics in Education*, pp197–231. London: Falmer Press.

Williams, R. and Yeomans, D. (1994) 'The New Vocationalism Enacted? The Transformation of the Business Studies Curriculum', *The Vocational Aspect*, **46**(3), 221–39.

Williams, R., Higham, J. and Yeomans, D. (1994) *External Evaluation of Rochdale TVEI: Final Report*. School of Education, University of Leeds.

Willis, P. (1977) *Learning to Labour*. Aldershot: Saxon House.

Young, M., Hayton, A., Hodgson, A. and Morris, A. (1994) 'An Interim Approach to Unifying the Post-16 Curriculum', in Tomlinson, S. (ed.) *Educational Reform and its Consequences*, pp73–92. London: Rivers Oram Press.

Index